Honest, Officer, The Midget Was On Fire When I Got Here

Ludlow Porch

On The Radio

LONGSTREET PRESS
Atlanta, Georgia

Dedication

*To Ed and Barbara Duffy,
my Yankee brother and sister*

Acknowledgment

*Special thanks
to my friend
William G. Sanders,
without whose help this book
would have been short*

*Published by
LONGSTREET PRESS, INC.
2150 Newmarket Parkway
Suite 102
Marietta, Georgia 30067*

Copyright © 1989 by Ludlow Porch

Printed in the United States of America

1st printing, 1989

Library of Congress Catalog Number 89-084526

ISBN 0-929264-62-2

This book was printed by Berryville Graphics, Berryville, Virginia, through Anderson, Barton & Dalby, Inc. The text was set in ITC Bookman by Typo-Repro Service, Inc., Atlanta, Georgia.

Illustrations by Mike Lester.

Talk Show

I am one of the luckiest men on the face of the earth. I have been allowed, for most of my adult life, to earn a living doing something that many people would do for free. I have my own talk radio show.

I have never known anyone who was ever in radio that has been completely happy doing anything else. I know doctors, lawyers, and professional jocks who would trade jobs with me in a heartbeat.

I'm not sure why it's such a fun job. I do know that when I'm on the air, the hours fly by, and I am on a high that few, if any other, jobs can equal.

I'm not saying it's not a high pressure job. Lord knows, it is! I have seen some very talented talk hosts fired because of one bad rating book. I have worked for some program directors who couldn't find their own fanny in a phone booth. And I have come to accept that in radio, like TV, the least creative people are always in charge of creativity.

With all of its drawbacks, however, it is still the world's best job.

I hope in the pages to follow that I will be able to give you some of the feeling of the fun and excitement that is the world of talk radio.

It's my world, and, God, how I do love it!

Oops!

The Rome, Georgia, newsman was reading the story about a trip that some local residents had taken to Mexico.

He meant to say, "The group had to cut their trip short, due to organisms in the water."

What he actually said was, "The group had to cut their trip short, due to orgasms in the water."

Mouths of Babes

When your job is talk radio, your life revolves around topics. If you pick good topics, you usually get good calls.

I am always looking for the next day's topics. I read books, magazines, even catalogs. I watch for topics on TV. I listen for topics while I'm standing in line at the Burger Doodle.

There are a few sure-fire topics, but none better than the one I call "Out of the Mouths of Babes." This topic consists of having the radio audience call in and tell stories about their children, grandchildren, or any child.

I have never failed to have a funny show once this topic is introduced. The following stories were all told as the truth, and who could doubt them?

A five-year-old and a seven-year-old were looking through a Sunday School book. The seven-year-old, being older and wiser, pointed to a picture and said, "That's a picture of Jesus." His five-year-old brother said, "Are you sure? Let me see that book. I betcha that's somebody else who works up there."

A mother overheard her two children talking about where babies come from. The youngest child had heard that babies come out of their mother's toe. The older child said, "Oh, don't be silly. Everybody knows babies come out of your Virginia."

The mother told her five-year-old to wash his hands before dinner. The little guy said, "My hands are clean." The mother said, "Go wash your hands—they have germs on them." Heading for the bathroom, the mother heard him say under his breath, "Germs and Jesus. That's all I ever hear about, and I ain't never seen neither one of them."

A seven-year-old boy was very happy with his newfound reading skill. One day he was trying to show his mom how much he was learning by reading the newspaper. He almost caused her to drop her teeth when he asked, "Mom, why doesn't Anita Bryant like homemakers?"

The three-year-old girl had wanted a baby sister. When the new arrival came, it turned out to be a boy. When her grandmother asked her how she liked her new brother, she said, "He's O. K., I guess, but there were things we needed a lot more."

The fourteen-year-old boy was shocked when his mother came into the bathroom while he was taking his shower. He was embarrassed and said, "Hey, Mom! I don't have any clothes on."

His mother said, "Don't be silly. I've seen you naked before."

"Yeah," the teen-ager said, "but not lately."

The two-year-old girl had been forbidden to touch the small porcelain horse that sat on the family coffee table. Finally, even though her father was watching, she couldn't resist any longer. She picked up the horse and dropped it, breaking it in half. She looked up at her silent but obviously furious dad and, in her wee, two-year-old voice, said, "Damn me!"

The police pulled a father over for speeding. The man's five-year-old was in the back seat, and the two and a half-year-old son was strapped into his car seat. When the policeman got to the car window, the five-year-old said, "Are you going to put us in jail?"

The two and a half-year-old said, "Shut up! He's got a gun!"

The three-year-old had done something to displease her mother. She was sent outside with instructions to bring back a switch. The child was gone for about ten minutes and came back with a rock in her little hand. She walked up to her mother and said, "I couldn't find a switch. Will this do?"

Children love jokes, but many times they can't get the punch line right.

The five-year-old had heard the following joke at kindergarten: "What did the Indian say when his dog fell off the cliff?" The Indian said, "Dog gone." It's not a very funny joke, but to this five-year-old it was wonderful. He could not wait to get home to tell his mother. He was afraid he wouldn't remember it, however, so all the way home he kept repeating it over and over to himself. He burst into the house and asked his mother, "What did the Indian say when his dog fell over the cliff?"

His mom said, "I don't know. What?"

"Dammit!" came the quick reply.

The four-year-old was in the car with his uncle. When the uncle flipped on his turn signal, the youngster said, "What is that ticking sound?"

His uncle said, "That's my turn signal."

"What's a turn signal?" asked the four-year-old.

The uncle said, "That's to let the other cars know that I'm turning." The child wrinkled his brow and said, "Ain't no way they're ever going to hear that!"

The eight-year-old boy asked his mother where babies came from. His mother considered herself to be progressive, so she spent about forty-five minutes explaining the facts of life to her son. When she was all through, he said, "Sounds a lot like mouth-to-mouth resuscitation to me."

The five-year-old asked his mother where he came from. The mother explained in terms she thought he could understand. When she finished, the little boy said, "My friend Jimmy is not going to like this."

"Why?" asked the mother.

The five-year-old said, "Because Jimmy doesn't like girls."

The little boy was attending the funeral of his beloved aunt. He was standing with his family as the first shovelful of dirt was thrown into the open grave. In a loud voice he said, "Well, that's the last we'll see of her."

A car pulled directly in front of a young mother and her four-year-old. Horns blew and tires skidded. When the emergency was over, the four-year-old said, "Mommy, that's not a sonofabitch. That's a Volkswagen."

Oops!

Bill Sanders on WKLY in Hartwell was trying to say, "Mrs. Herman Wilkins died today in a rest home in Toccoa."

What came out was, "Mrs. Herman Wilkins died today in a restroom in Toccoa."

The Dump Button

To do live talk radio, it is necessary to operate on a delay system. This simply means that the audience hears what has been said six seconds later than it was actually spoken.

In the event a caller says something that is not suitable for the public airways, the host has six seconds to hit the "dump button" and delete the objectionable comment.

Some of the funniest things ever said on radio never are heard outside the booth because the host or producer was able to cut them out.

I will never forget the time when my topic was, "What is the government doing for you that you want them to stop?"

The lines were full of people making very serious comments about the government sticking its nose into their lives.

I put a caller on the line, and, in a very serious voice, he said, "Ludlow, the Navy must be made to stop putting saltpeter into our sailors' food."

Like the unsuspecting clown I was, I asked, "Why?"

He said, "Because they gave me some in 1943, and it's just now starting to work."

I hit the "dump button" and moved on to the next call. The lady on the line was laughing her head off. I said, "What are you laughing at?"

She said, "I think I know that guy."

I have one nut who has been calling me about once a week for ten years. When I answer the phone, all he says is, "Do-do." I, of course, hit the "dump button" and immediately hang up on him.

This must be the most determined pervert on the face of the earth because the next week he calls back with the same routine. He does not seem to mind that for ten years he has been trying to say "do-do" on the radio, and, to date, nobody in radioland has ever even heard his voice.

I have considered letting him say it and get it out of his twisted little system. I decided, however, to continue to dump him, since, as a talk show host, I hate to lose a regular caller.

I had a guest on several years ago to discuss a play he had written that was a big hit. To say my guest was a little light in the loafers was giving him the benefit of every doubt. The fact of the matter is that this old boy was much, much more feminine than Audrey Hepburn.

He did not seem to be interested in talking about his play, but, rather, preferred to talk about "gay rights." Every time I would ask a question about the play, his answer would have something to do with the fact that he was gay and proud of it. When I started taking calls, the callers were quick to condemn his life style, and he was just as quick to call them close-minded bigots.

Finally, an elderly lady called and started out her comment by saying, "I am a Christian." I have learned, over the years, that means the caller is about to say something very un-Christian. This call was no exception.

You could feel the hate in her voice as she started to lecture my guest. I said, "Ma'am, you said you were a Christian, but it sounds to me like you hate this man."

She shouted back, "I don't hate anybody, but this man should be down on his knees praying."

In a high-pitched, quivering voice, my guest shot back, "Lady, when I get on my knees, I've got better things to do than pray!"

Thank God for that wonderful little "dump button."

There have been two occasions when I had to hit the "dump button" on myself. (There have been about two thousand occasions when I should have and didn't.)

Skip Caray, the very talented voice of the Atlanta Braves, dedicated his life, for awhile, to breaking me up on the air. In the late 1970s, Skip and I worked together at the old Ring Radio, WRNG in Atlanta. One of our sponsors was the Honeybaked Ham Company.

In those days, all of the Honeybaked Ham spots were read live. The last line in the commercial read, "Honeybaked — the ham so good it will haunt you till it's gone." We had been given instructions to read that last line with a great deal of feeling and sincerity.

I was reading the spot one day when Skip came silently into the broadcast booth behind me. I didn't hear him, and I had no idea he was there. When I came to the all-important last line in the commercial, Skip gave me a big, wet kiss in the ear. I probably could have handled that,

14

but when his lips were about a quarter-inch away from my ear, static electricity arced between us. I got a sharp shock in my ear, followed by a big, wet kiss. This is the way the commercial ended: "Honeybaked — the ham so good it will — JESUS CHRIST!"

People called the front desk for two hours asking why we had bleeped our own commercial. We never told a soul — until now.

We had a news anchor at Ring Radio named Brenda. In addition to being a very talented news person, Brenda had been richly blessed by Mother Nature. She was very well built and did more for a sweater than "Izod." As I was on the air one day, I looked up and saw the shapely Brenda outside the studio, looking through the glass, eating a very large and juicy pear.

Without thinking twice, I said into the open mike, "Brenda has the biggest pear I have ever seen."

It was an innocent remark, and I did not realize I had said anything wrong until Brenda spit pear juice all over the glass window and my producer fell out of his chair. Fortunately, he hit the "dump button" before he lost consciousness.

Oops!

On WSB-FM, singer-songwriter Barry Manilow was introduced one day as "Barely Man Enough."

Montana

I guess the only person to get more publicity out of the State of Montana than me was General George Custer. But neither one of us had much hair when it was all over.

I was on the air, having an open line. We were talking about several different topics. A lady called and said that she had been in Atlanta on vacation and had become addicted to talk radio. She said that vacation time was about over, and they were on their way home. She went on to say that there was no talk radio where she lived, and she was going to miss it.

"Where are you from?" I asked.

She said, "We live in Montana."

"Don't give me that, Lady," I said. "I happen to know that there's no such place as Montana."

She said, "Why would you say a thing like that?"

I answered, "I've never been to Montana. I've never even met anyone who's been to Montana. As a matter of fact, I've never even seen a license plate from Montana, and, as far as I'm concerned, it doesn't exist. And my personal opinion is that the whole thing is some kind of government plot."

She laughed about it, and I laughed about it, we said our good-byes and hung up.

The switchboard suddenly lit up like a used car lot. I could not believe it, but people were calling me in droves, trying their very best to reason with me about the great state of Montana. They were serious. They really felt that I didn't believe a whole state existed. By this time, I was having fun.

I accused all of them of working for the CIA and being personally involved in the plot. I accused one caller of being a left wing, commie pinko bedwetter.

When I got off the air, I really felt the Montana show was over once and for all. I have never been more wrong.

The phone in my office was ringing a mile a minute, and the front switchboard was jammed with people wanting to talk to me about Montana. They were well armed with their facts:

• Their brother-in-law was stationed there during the war.

• They went through there once on a train.

• They were looking at a *World Book*, and it said the capital was. . . .

On and on the calls came. I never admitted that I had been kidding. I couldn't believe the reaction I was getting, but I knew that something very, very funny was happening.

The next day I went on the air, all set to talk about something else. Fat chance. As soon as my voice went on the air, the phones lit up. Everybody wanted to argue with me about Montana.

I realized at that point that I had gone too far to back out. For better or worse, Montana was going to be my topic for the next few weeks.

I reached a decision that night. If they wanted to talk about Montana, then I would really give them something to talk about.

Next morning I took my wife by my friend Tom Deardorf's house. I had prepared three scripts, and we all held a little early morning rehearsal.

I went on the air at eleven o'clock. I said, "O.K. Enough is enough. I have been trying to tell you people about this plot by our government, but all I'm getting for my efforts are crank phone calls and insulting letters." I said, "Did you people out there learn nothing at all from Watergate?

Our government is involved in a plot, and nobody out there seems willing to face the facts." I went on, "There is only one thing left to do. I'm going to call the Bureau of Archives in Washington, D.C., and talk to a real live walking, talking bureaucrat."

With that introduction, I dialed my friend's home number. The audience could hear his phone ringing. Right on cue, my wife answered the phone. In a very businesslike manner, she said, "Bureau of Archives."

In an equally businesslike manner, I said, "May I speak to the person who is in charge of the Montana Myth?" She shot back, "You must want our Lost and Found Department." I explained to her that we were on the air and I needed to talk to the person in charge of P.R. for the State of Montana.

She said, "You need to speak to our Mr. Walter Brown. He has been in charge of P.R. for the State of Montana for the past twenty-three years, and he can give you any information you need."

She put me on hold, and in about ten seconds my friend answered the phone. In a flat, low voice, he said, "Brown."

I said, "Mr. Brown, my name is Ludlow Porch, and you are on the air in Atlanta, Georgia." I then went on to tell him that we were checking on the existence of the State of Montana.

When I had finished, he went absolutely crazy. He said, "I cannot believe that any radio station would waste valuable airtime with such a stupid, off-the-wall telephone call like this. Does Montana exist?" he screamed. "Of course, it exists. I have been handling their P.R. for twenty-three years. I have been there hundreds of times. I have maps on my walls. I'm on a first name basis with the governor, and I don't have time to discuss this stupidity with some sicko on the radio!"

I asked him several more questions, and the more we talked, the more irritated he became.

Finally, I said, "Mr. Brown, it is apparent to me that you are not going to tell us anything more about the Montana plot. But, before we go, do you have any comment you'd care to make regarding the 1956 war between Oregon and Canada?" Suddenly there was silence on the line. In about fifteen seconds he came back in a very halting voice and said, "How . . . how . . . did you know about that?"

I said, "Let's get one thing straight, Brown. This is not one of your dummies from the *Washington Post* calling. This is Ludlow Porch from Snellville, Georgia, and we know about the Montana Plot."

He started to cry—not just to cry, but to blubber into the phone. In a slow, sad, sobbing voice he said, "Twenty-three years of faithful service, and my whole world is over with one lousy phone call." Still sobbing, he went on, "What will I tell my wife? How will I pay for my children's education? My job is gone. What will I do? Where will I work?"

I said, "Pull yourself together, man! We are going to give you a chance to stop living a lie. You don't have to work for the government. You can get a decent, honest job pumping gas at a Gulf station!"

It was at this point that he broke down and admitted the whole thing.

There had been a war in 1956 between Oregon and Canada. Oregon had lost, and the U.S. Government had been so embarrassed they had covered up the war. The battleground area was called Montana. He admitted that Montana did not exist, had never existed, and the whole thing was a government plot.

He was still blubbering into the phone when I wished him my warmest personal regards, apologized for ruining his life, and hung up on him.

I was really not prepared for what came next. I really thought that this time I was finished talking about the Big Sky State. I thought that anybody listening would know that the whole thing was a spoof and that would be that. Wrong again!

My conversation with the fake bureaucrat was over at 11:40. In the next forty minutes, by actual count, over twenty thousand people tried to call me on the air.

To my complete and absolute amazement, thousands of people had taken the whole thing seriously. The telephone company actually called my program director to complain about the volume of calls.

Not everyone was taken in, however. A lot of people knew it was a spoof, and they were just calling in to be a part of it. One man called and said that he was the salesman who had sold silencers to both sides during the Oregon-Canadian War.

Others didn't think the spoof was as funny as I did. One man could not get through on the air, but he was so mad he called our front switchboard. He told the receptionist, "You tell that S.O.B. that I just dialed the area code for Montana, and, *by God*, they answered!"

United Press International heard about what was going on and sent a reporter to talk to me. His name was Charles Taylor, and he was as amazed as I was by the response we were receiving. He wrote a story, put it on the UPI wire, and it went coast to coast.

In the next forty-eight hours I did telephone interviews on radio and TV talk shows all over the country.

I stuck to my guns. Not one time did I admit that I had pulled a spoof. I told some of the God-awfullest lies that had ever been told.

I received over five hundred pieces of mail that first week.

I made the front page of not one but two Montana newspapers.

I received a package from the Montana Department of Roads and Travel. It was full of every map ever made of the state of Montana.

I got a letter from the Secretary of State of Montana. He was not amused.

I received a call from a newspaper columnist in Florida. I could tell by the tone of his voice that he really thought I was serious about the Montana thing. This well-educated, experienced newspaper man really thought I was trying to convince the world that a whole state did not exist. I decided that it might be fun to put the old boy on.

He started the interview with a couple of simple questions. Then he got to the tough ones. He said, "Mr. Porch, if there is not such a place as Montana, how do you explain the existence of Senator Mike Mansfield?"

I said, "People in this country have been trying to explain Senator Mansfield for twenty years, but you, Sir, are in luck, because I can do it." Without even pausing to take a breath, I said,

"The man you know as Mike Mansfield is actually an actor, who is employed by the CIA to go to Washington when the Senate is in session and pose as the senior senator from Montana. His real name," I added, "is LeRoy Ferguson. And when the Senate is not in session, he is the assistant line coach at a high school located right here in North Georgia."

I heard his typewriter go into overdrive. He said, "What was that name again?" I shot back with conviction, "LeRoy Ferguson."

There was a short pause, and he said in a rather subdued voice, "Mr. Porch, can you prove that?"

I said, "Of course, I can prove it. Have you ever seen a picture of LeRoy Ferguson and Mike Mansfield together?"

He finally got the idea that I was pulling his leg. We laughed about it, and he wrote a nice column and sent me a copy.

I received a long distance call from radio station WAIT in Chicago. They wanted to know if I would come to the Windy City and talk about Montana. I got on an airplane, and away I went.

A funny thing happened in Chicago. When I had talked about this around the South and Southeast, people had tried to reason with me. They had tried to explain it to me in calm, rational terms. In Chicago it made them mad. It made them very, very mad.

I'm not sure why, but I have thought about it, and the only thing I can figure is that if you live in an area that has two seasons, winter and the Fourth of July, it tends to make you irritable.

The host of the show introduced me, and for about fifteen minutes I gave her my stock lies about Montana. She knew it was a spoof but never let on to her audience.

The third or fourth call we received on the air was from a man who was really angry. He said he worked at a post office in Chicago and had for more than eighteen years. He said that in that time, he had seen thousands of letters, postcards, and packages with Montana addresses, return addresses, and postmarks.

He was so angry that his voice was getting louder and louder. He said, "I don't know how a major radio station could have this redneck cracker on the air." His voice was also getting more vicious as he went on to say, "The FCC should take that radio station's license away, and we should ride that redneck out of town on a rail, back to those ugly red clay hills where he came from!"

When he finally took a breath, I said, "Did you say you worked for the post office?"

He said, "Damn right!"

I said, "Who dialed the phone for you?"

The man went crazy and finally had to be cut off by my host.

When I got back home, the mail had piled up from all over the U.S.

I was amazed at how people had reacted to the Montana spoof. I had received hundreds and hundreds of letters from people who really believed I was serious.

This was my first spoof. It was not my last. Read on.

Oops!

On Z-93 in Atlanta, the female D.J. meant to say, "Listen for your chance to win in the ten-thousand-dollar jackpot."

What she said was, "Listen for your chance to win in the ten-thousand-dollar jackoff."

Naugas

I was in a restaurant one day for lunch. It was late, and I was about the only customer.

A salesman was trying to talk the owner of the place into putting new Naugahyde on all her chairs and barstools.

I thought to myself, "I wonder how many Naugas it takes to cover one chair?" The idea struck me as kind of funny, so I starting putting another spoof together. It took me about a week to arrange the whole show.

On the day of the spoof, I got my buddy Tom Deardorf to come to the station to do the voice of my Imaginary Guest. I opened the mike and made my intro. I said, "If there is anyone out there in radioland who would like to make some extra money and enjoy a fun hobby, leave your dial right where it is. My special guest today is in town selling franchises, so have your pen and paper ready to jot down his name and address. I'm pleased to have with me today the world's largest raiser and breeder of Naugas, Mr. Harvey Weems, and he is here to tell you the benefits of raising Naugas for fun and profit."

I had decided to make my Nauga spoof so far out that nobody listening would believe a word of what we were saying. I said that raising Naugas is a highly profitable business for three very important reasons:

1. The only thing they eat is ground-up Clorox bottles.

2. If you are careful you can skin a Nauga without killing it.

3. The female Nauga has an hour and twenty-five minute gestation period.

No. 3 was the one that started the phones to ringing.

We went on to say that my guest had been cross-breeding and had developed a plaid-colored Nauga. Not only that, but he had been able to breed them with zippers in their little bellies, so you could unzip them and put their skins directly on sofa cushions.

To my amazement, people were calling to get more information from my guest. Thousands of people really wanted to be Nauga ranchers. They wanted to find out how to write for more information, how much they cost a pair, etc.

Not everybody believed it, however. One man called and said, "I have been a hunter all my life. Why have I never seen a Nauga in the wild?" I explained that by telling him Naugas were the world's most shy animal.

When he didn't buy my lie, I said, "Have you ever seen a cashew in the wild?"

He said, "No."

I said, "But you believe they exist, don't you?" The cashew reference for some reason seemed to satisfy him.

One caller was curious about the fact that the female had a one hour and twenty-five minute gestation period.

"How do they breed?" he asked.

I said, "Nobody knows."

He shot back, "What do you mean 'Nobody knows'?"

I said, "They are so fast you have to throw them in the cage and get the hell out of the way."

In the next few weeks I received several hundred letters and phone calls asking for the address of Mr. Weems so listeners could write him for more information.

As strange as it seems, I got letters and phone calls from potential Nauga ranchers for about five years.

Oops!

The Alabama announcer was reading the funeral notices on the air.

In a solemn tone he said, "Services for Mrs. Thomas will be at three P.M. tomorrow, with burial at the Alexander City Shopping Center."

H.E.W.

My favorite target over the years has been the government. When you do humor full time, you soon learn to watch the newspapers to find out what the folks in government are up to.

If you pay close attention, you soon learn that the government does some funny stuff. The folks at Health, Education and Welfare, for example, are funnier than a drunk possum.

It seemed to me that those folks were overly concerned with what they like to call "guidelines."

It also seemed to me that they were just sitting there on their gold throne, all set to drop like a load of cordwood on anybody they thought might be outside one of their little old guidelines.

I had a man on my show one day whom I introduced as a field agent for H.E.W. He was, in fact, a drunken Irish friend of mine who came by the radio station to get out of the rain.

I told my radio audience that this H.E.W. official was in Atlanta to open a field office.

I went on to say that H.E.W., in their wisdom, had determined that the marriage licenses issued in the seven southeastern states (and certain parts of Florida) since 1968 were outside the Marriage License Guidelines, as set down by H.E.W. Therefore, all the marriages performed in those states since 1968 were null and void.

I have no idea how many phone calls we got on the air about this one, but I know the phones at the radio station were in great danger of melting. The bulk of the calls were from people who were worried about their children and grandchildren being born out of wedlock.

The most interesting call I received was from a man who identified himself as an official of H.E.W. He was so mad his voice was trembling. He said H.E.W. had received several thousand phone calls about my spoof, and they had not been able to get any work done in their office in three days. I asked him how he could tell. He was not amused. The longer we talked, the more outraged he became.

When I was convinced that the poor man was only seconds away from a complete nervous breakdown, I said, "Hold on just a minute. I don't want any trouble with the government. If you will give me until tomorrow, I promise I will go on the air and get this whole thing straightened out."

He was still screaming when he said, "You damn well better get it straightened out!" and he slammed the phone in my ear.

I hate it when a government worker can't take a joke.

The next day I went on the air and, in a very serious voice, said, "I don't want you people out there calling H.E.W. anymore because you are getting me in a lot of trouble."

I said, "I have not slept all night. I have been in meetings with officials of H.E.W., officials of the state, and the manager of this radio station, and I am pleased to announce that they have agreed to allow me to hold the largest mass wedding in the history of mankind."

I went on, "Now, here's the way this is going to work. I want you to take your old, invalid marriage license back to the courthouse where you bought it originally. You should turn it in to the county clerk, and he will give you a new one, at no cost, of course. Then, I want you and your beloved to be by your radio with your new marriage license next Thursday. We are bringing in at great expense to the radio station the world renowned evangelist The Reverend Anthony Slatz of the Dunk and Dine Baptist Church, Route #3, New Hope, Tennessee."

I explained the ceremony would start at exactly 11:15.

When you hear the organ music start, put your new marriage license on the table in front of your radio, then hold hands with your intended and put your other hand on the radio, and we, Dear Hearts, are going to marry you."

I can't be sure, of course, but I think the H.E.W. man was madder the second time he called than he was the first.

I guess I should feel bad about all the fun I have poked at the government over the years, but, somehow, I just can't.

I only wish they had enjoyed it as much as I have.

Oops!

Lowell Thomas was reading the story about how the world's fattest lady had lost over five hundred pounds.

He said, "Her doctors told her she must lose weight after she suffered a near fartel heart attack."

Naughty Talk

I do a thing on the air every once in awhile that I call "Letters to Ludlow." It works a little like "Dear Abby," except that Abby gets real letters, and I make mine up.

I just write myself a letter, sign a phony name to it, read it on the air, and ask my audience for their comments. No matter how off the wall I make my letters, I always get very interesting calls.

I read the following letter on the air:

Dear Ludlow:
    I just read in the local paper that the federal government is about to give $2.5

million to promote theater art in our
area. I have checked into this, and
frankly, I am outraged.

A recent survey has shown that over
ninety percent of the people in our area
involved in the theater are known practicing thespians. Ludlow, this is a dis-
grace. I don't care what these wretched
creatures do in the privacy of their own
homes, but to use tax money is going
absolutely too far!

Please let your radio audience know that
our tax money is being used on
thespians.

Just sign me . . .
Outraged in Oakland City

I read the letter on the air and watched the
phones light up. I have always been amazed at
the number of people who will call a talk show
and try to make a comment when they are not
real sure what we are talking about.

One of the first calls I received was from a lady
who said, "We should try and be more tolerant of
thespians. After all, they can't help it. They are
born that way."

Another woman called and said there were many new treatments nowadays and that psychiatrists were having great success treating thespians.

She closed her conversation by saying, "With medical science being what it is today, you don't have to be a thespian if you don't want to be."

One man, who had figured out what I was up to, called to get in on the fun. He said, in a very serious tone of voice, "I have it on very good authority that John Wayne was a practicing thespian for well over fifty years."

I shot right back, "Hold on a second, Buster. John Wayne was a great American. John Wayne was a credit to his mama and daddy. And if you think I'm going to sit here and listen to you besmirch the Duke's good name, you are out of your evil mind!" Then I hung up on him.

In the course of the next two hours, I talked to about twenty-five people who had no idea what a thespian was but nevertheless wanted to talk about our topic.

I think there is a lesson to be learned here, and it was summed up by the call our general manager received from one irate lady. She said, "I don't know what it means, but I know you shouldn't be talking about it on the radio."

Oops!

What Jim Rich of WBIE meant to say was, "The United Textile Workers."

What came out was, "The United Testicle Workers."

Governor Griffin

Marvin Griffin was a former Lieutenant Governor and a former Governor of Georgia before I ever met him. I don't remember much about his politics, but I can attest to the fact that he was one of the all-time funny characters.

One election year, long after he had retired from politics, he was hired by an Atlanta TV station to be their election night analyst/expert. He was to sit there with the TV newsman and comment on the returns as they poured in. This was in the days before networks forecast the winner within fifteen or twenty minutes of the polls' closing.

Shortly after midnight, the vote-a-matic

machines in DeKalb County broke down, and since no returns were coming in, there was nothing for the TV news guy and Governor Griffin to do except to try and fill some time.

They talked about every aspect of the election. They filled on and on. The whole time, Governor Griffin was chain-smoking cigarettes. Finally, in a desperate effort to fill even more time, the newsman turned to Governor Griffin and said, "Governor, has there ever been a time in your adult life when you did not want a cigarette?"

Lighting another one, he said, "As a matter of fact, there was just such a time. My brother Chaney and me was fishing down on Lake Sinclair. We had been out on that bass boat about four hours in the hot sun. Fortunately," he went on, "Chaney had the foresight and good sense to bring along a cooler full of ice cold beer, and we had been sipping along on that beer most of the day.

"Along about dinner time, I received a call from Mother Nature. It was a direct result of drinkin' all that beer." Taking another long draw on his cigarette, he continued. "I walked there to the bow of that boat to answer Mother Nature's call about the same time Chaney was gettin' ready to cast."

He said, "I'll never forget it if I live to be a hundred years old. Chaney was using one of them doodlebug lures. It was a fearsome-looking thing, with hooks all over it. Just about the time I started to answer Nature's call, old Chaney cast and caught me in a very, very strategic area. And, to answer your question, for the next thirty seconds I did not want a cigarette."

Oops!

The Georgia Tech play-by-play announcer started his broadcast in a very dramatic way. He opened the mike and said:

GRANT FIELD . . . ATLANTA, GEORGIA . . . (pause) CHECK THAT . . . THE COLISEUM . . . LOS ANGELES, CALIFORNIA.

The Whackos

I have been asked many times, "What is a whacko?" I'm not sure I really know, but I will try one more time to explain.

Like every talk show host in the country, I have a host of regular callers. For years I have referred to my regulars as "my whackos." It is a term I use very lovingly because they are a group of very funny, creative people who like to get on the air and release their humor on all of mankind.

Over the years, we have somehow given all of them names—names like Leather Britches, Kitty Litter, Sparky, Beef Jerky, Miss Sarah, Humphrey of Bogart, and Ray D. Ator.

I'm not sure exactly how many whackos there

are, but once we had a whacko party and over five thousand people showed up.

The whackos have all had their high moments on the air. I'll never forget the time Leather Britches called with this riddle: "What are the last three words you want to hear when you're making love?" "Honey, I'm home!"

I'm not sure how long Erlene has been a whacko, but it's well over ten years. She always starts her call the same way: "This is Erlene P. Bountiful, world's only country-western exotic dancer. The *P* stands for precious and plentiful."

One day she called and, in her high-pitched voice, announced that she had a new receipt for sweet potatoes. She called them her "Wham Bam Thank You Yam" receipt.

Erlene is very proud of the fact that she is the *only* country-western exotic dancer in the world. She claims her favorite outfit is pasties and a G-string. She also claims to be very much into streaking, although she doesn't call it streaking. She calls it running naked.

For years my signoff has been, "Whatever else you do today, find somebody to be nice to." Erlene has her signoff, as well. She says, "Whatever else you do today, find somebody to get naked with."

One of the newer whackos calls himself Luther Phillips. Luther claims to be 104 years old, and on the phone Luther sounds like he is at least that old.

Luther lives at a place he refers to only as "The Home." To say Luther has an "eye for the ladies" would be a gross understatement. It would be much more accurate to say Luther, in spite of his age, never seems to get his mind above his belt buckle.

He is romantically involved with a shapely eighteen-year-old named Buffy.

He is too old to do a lot of driving, so an orderly from the home drives him around.

He once told me on the air that every night three orderlies take him to Buffy's house, and in the morning four orderlies come to take him back to the home. I said, "Luther, why does it take only three to take you there at night and four to pick you up in the morning?"

Quick as a wink he replied, "'Cause I fight 'em!"

Luther claims to live in the nudist wing at "The Home." He told me the story about the time they had a flower show in the nudist wing and he won a blue ribbon for "best dried arrangement."

Luther also told me about the time he answered the phone and a woman's voice said, "You old fool! You got me pregnant!" Luther said, "Who is this?"

Like many of the whackos, Luther has his own signoff. He says, "To all the women out there, you got to make love to somebody, and I need the action."

What else can you say about a 104-year-old man who just got a tattoo that says, "Born to Raise Hell"?

Pony is a lovely lady and a rural mail carrier. She is more of an animal lover than Tarzan. When she finds a turtle crossing the road, she stops, gets out of her car, and helps Mr. Turtle to the other side.

Her house is full of dogs and cats that she has rescued and is trying to find homes for. She once picked up a three-legged dog that she named Tripod.

She called on the air one day and said that she had found another three-legged dog and wanted the radio audience to come up with a name for it. Many listeners responded. The dog was named when our ace newsman Dave Foulk called and suggested the name Ilean.

A whacko who claims to be "the mayor of Lost Mountain" has a delightful dry wit that absolutely knocks me out. He likes to call and read me letters from his mama, who lives in Fargo, Georgia.

He read me a letter once about the Rattlesnake Roundup that is held every year in Fargo. It seems that a local man got drunk and was riding his motorcycle around the pit where the rattlesnakes were being kept.

He was so drunk that he had accidentally set his hair on fire and in his hysteria drove his Harley right into the pit of rattlesnakes. When they finally dragged him out of the pit, he had been bitten 178 times. The mayor's mama said it was the first recorded case in the state of Georgia of a man being the victim of a "fang bang."

M.T. Head bills himself as "Georgia's only auto mechanic and brain surgeon and the only graduate of Shorty's Agricultural, Mechanical and Medical School, Pit Bar-B-Q Cafe and Truck Stop, Letohatchie, Alabama, 36047." M.T. is one of the funniest men I have ever known.

One day we were talking about unlucky things. Several people had called and said that black cats crossing your path were unlucky. M.T. called and said that black cats crossing your path were not unlucky. What was unlucky was when a black cat stopped in your path and said, "Give me all your money, sucker."

Bloody Mary has been a whacko for over fifteen years. We lovingly refer to her as our "resident drunk." She has not had a drink in about three or four years, but there was a time when she could drink with the best of them.

Bloody Mary is a natural wit. Even sober, she looks at the world from a different point of view than other folks.

Several years ago I was on the air on Thanksgiving Day. Mary called and seemed to be a little upset. I said, "Mary, you don't sound like you are enjoying Thanksgiving."

She said, "Oh! It's this damn turkey."

I said, "Are you having trouble with your holiday turkey?"

"Yeah. When I started cooking, I basted the turkey with a quart of vodka."

"Really? Did it ruin it?"

She said, "I don't know. The turkey keeps opening the oven door and turning down the heat."

Norman is one of our resident whackos. He calls once a week and gives us his words to live by. He claims to be an everyday, garden variety philosopher.

He always says he is calling from his favorite rocking chair in front of his fireplace. He is wearing a houndstooth hat, has a shawl around his shoulders, and is smoking a pipe. He also claims to be wearing bedroom slippers with Indian heads on them. His pet pig, Blue, is sleeping peacefully at his feet.

Norman speaks in a very low, wise-sounding voice. Following are some of his better pieces of work:

Hard times are when the bird singing outside your window is a buzzard.

Old men look at the past, while young men look at what's passing.

Your temper improves the more you don't use it.

Don't pray for rain and then complain about the mud.

A nudist doesn't have to hold out his hand to see if it's raining.

The problem with humor is that people take it seriously.

Eskimos are God's frozen People.

The cheaper the wine, the easier it is to pronounce.

Life holds no greater delight for a father than overhearing his son say, "My dad can."

The youngest, who knows the value of a dollar, will usually ask for two.

A madam is a woman who dispenses vice to the lovelorn.

Fame is largely a matter of dying at the right moment.

The most optimistic person I ever heard of was Solomon's five hundredth wife.

The only way to fight a woman is with your hat. Grab it and run.

Novelty is a lawyer with his hands in his own pocket.

Most of the future lies ahead.

Laziness is resting before you get tired.

A key chain permits you to lose several keys at the same time.

A trial marriage is a very dangerous thing. If you're not careful, it could lead to the real thing.

You can live happily ever after, if you ain't after too much.

Stupid people shouldn't breed.

You're ugly if you go into a bank and they turn the cameras off.

The secret for a long life is to walk softly, speak wisely, and carry a concealed weapon.

Ninety percent of the game is mental, and the other half is physical.

If you don't make mistakes, you might live and die without ever hearing your name mentioned.

The road to success is dotted with many tempting parking spaces.

More diets start in a dress shop than in a doctor's office.

If tombstones told the truth, everybody would want to be buried at sea.

Even if the world is your oyster, you have to open the shell yourself.

The secret of success is learning at an early age that you are not God.

I lived in a neighborhood that was so tough any girl not on penicillin was considered a debutante.

Drinking and chasing women don't mix. You start staggering, and they get away.

Early to bed and early to rise, till you make enough cash to do otherwise.

One of the most popular time savers is yielding to temptation right away.

Alimony is like buying a ticket to an amusement park and finding all the rides are closed.

The economy is so bad in my hometown that last week three hookers were arrested, and two of them were virgins.

One of the most popular whackos is Ciro Greenburg. Ciro claims to be the owner of the only drive-in funeral home in the Southeast. He calls it the B.B.C. (Bodies by Ciro).

The B.B.C. is a closed Burger King that Ciro has converted to a full-service funeral home. He is very proud of the fact that while you're waiting in line to view the dearly departed, you can have your car greased and your oil changed. He also serves jalapeno dip in the lobby.

Ciro has three young ladies at the B.B.C. to give comfort to the bereaved — Bunny, Evelyn, and Merlene. He calls them the "grief ladies."

For a fee, they will scatter your ashes from an airplane. Ciro calls this his Aerial Burial, or, "Blowing in the Wind."

Milton Crabapple is a caller who sounds exactly, and I mean exactly, like Walter Brennan. I guess every show biz impressionist has done Walter Brennan at one time or another, but none of them, including Rich Little, sounds as much like him as Milton.

He refers to me only as "that gol-durn Ludlow."

One day we were talking about politicians. We had several calls from people who said they wanted stronger gun control from their elected officials. One man called and said he was tired of all the Bible quoting from politicians.

Milton called and said his ideal elected official would be a man with a Bible in one hand and a gun in the other—who knew how to use them both.

Milton Crabapple is a little confused about living in the twentieth century. He called one day and said he was going on vacation. I asked, "Where you goin', Milton?" He said he was going to visit his sister in Pepsi-Cola, Florida. He was a little uneasy about flying. He said he was afraid them "gol-dang Russians" was going to try and get back at us for shootin' down them two Lesbian fighter planes.

Some of the best lines I have ever heard came on the air from whackos.

A man called once with this advice: "Never pick up hot dishes with small house pets."

One day a man called and said, "Ludlow, I have a riddle for you."

I said, "I'm not very good at riddles, but I'll try."

He said, "What do you get when you cross Lassie with a pit bull?"

I didn't know. He said, "You get a dog that will tear your leg off and then go for help."

A caller described his friend by saying, "He is so ugly he looks like his face has worn out three bodies."

A lady called and complained once that she had the world's ugliest children. I said, "How ugly are they?"

She said, "Ludlow, my children are so ugly that when we make home movies we hire stand-ins for the children."

One day some of my regular callers got into a friendly argument about who made the better car—Ford or Chevrolet. The topper came when an elderly gentleman called from the North Georgia mountains and said, "Ludlow, I've been buying cars for over sixty years, and I would rather walk up a ditch carrying a Ford hubcap than own the best Chevrolet ever made."

I guess the thing that makes my job so exciting is the fact that you never know what kind of wonderful surprise is waiting for you behind that blinking telephone light.

Oops!

The network announcer intended to say, "A Tale of Two Cities." What he actually said was, "A Sale of Two Titties."

The Contest

Radio Station WDUN in Gainesville, Georgia, was looking for a way to draw a crowd of local citizens together and, at the same time, help boost their ratings.

Gainesville proudly calls itself "The Poultry Capital of The World," so it seemed only natural to have a chicken-eating contest on the air.

The contest was to be held at the Civic Center, with a large crowd acting as a studio audience.

The host of the show was my friend Bill Sanders, and to help hype the whole thing, the station brought in the then voice of the Atlanta Braves, Milo Hamilton, to act as Bill's co-host.

I can't imagine anyone more out of place at a

chicken-eating contest than Milo Hamilton. He was a very talented play-by-play announcer. He also had an ego the size of Waco, Texas. The only one-word description I could give of Hamilton would be "pompous."

The first prize was to be $100 in cash and several gift certificates from local Gainesville merchants. The chicken was being prepared and furnished by the local Kentucky Fried Chicken store.

It was a gala event, and the chicken eaters came from miles around.

One of the contestants was a good old boy from Cumming, Georgia, named Junior Samples. Junior went on to become one of the stars of the television show "Hee-Haw," but at this point in his life, no one outside of his hometown had ever heard of him.

The contest went on and on. One by one, the other contestants dropped out, but not old Junior. When the contest was over, he had eaten sixty pieces of Kentucky Fried Chicken.

A great cheer went up from the crowd when Junior was declared the winner.

Milo Hamilton, wearing a $300 suit, approached Junior with microphone in hand, all set to interview the winner. He was just about to congratulate him when Mr. Samples threw up all over the mike.

I don't know how it sounded to the radio audience, but Milo was horrified to the point of not being able to speak. He just stood there holding the mike, saying, "Oh! Oh! Oh! Oh!"

It was obvious to even a casual observer that Mr. Hamilton had never been vomited on before.

Bill Sanders was close by and noticed that Hamilton was in no shape to continue, so he took the mike and finished the show.

I guess Murphy was right: if something can go wrong, it will.

Oops!

The master of ceremonies was about to introduce the world-famous banjo player Eddie Peabody.

He meant to say, "And, now, ladies and gentlemen, here is Eddie Peabody, who will now play for us."

What he said was, "And, now, ladies and gentlemen, here is Eddie Playbody, who will now pea for us."

Teenage Radio

In small towns all across America, it is not uncommon at all for teenage boys and girls to have their own radio shows. Some of the most famous names in radio and TV started out as teenagers on their hometown radio stations.

The stories that are told about some of the things that happen on these shows are told and retold anytime broadcasters get together.

One of my favorites happened in Hartwell, Georgia, at station WKLY.

Every weekend the station ran the "Obituary Column of the Air," when they announced who had passed away in the community that week. The announcer one weekend was my friend Bill

Sanders, who was fourteen or fifteen years old at the time.

The station had allotted four and one-half minutes for the obituaries.

The organ music of Jessie Crawford came on, and Bill, in his most grown-up voice, said, "The Pruett Herring Funeral Home brings you The Obituary Column of the Air. Today we pay reverence to the memory of. . . ."—pause—"We regret to announce that no one died this week."

This was followed by four minutes of absolute silence.

The Atlanta TV weekend anchor man concluded one dramatic news story with, "The teen-age girls escaped the fire with minor birds."

Part-Timers

On smaller radio stations, weekends are the time you put new folks on the air.

It's not that stations think weekends are unimportant. It's just that not as many people are listening, and it's a good time to let your full-timers off and give some less experienced folks a chance.

On Sunday, it is not unusual at all to find only one employee in a radio station, and, likely as not, that person could be very inexperienced.

That's why some of the best radio stories happen on the weekend.

This story took place at WRGA in Rome, Georgia. It was Sunday, and the news director had just left the station after his last newscast of the day.

Alone in the station was a part-timer who was just supposed to spin records and give the time and temperature between records.

Meanwhile, seventy miles south of Rome at the Georgia Radio Information News Network, another weekend part-timer was also alone at the network. He checked the UPI wire and saw the following story:

Dateline: Rome — Prince Philip visited Rome today. The prince and the Communist Mayor of Rome are going grouse hunting tomorrow on the outskirts of the city.

The part-timer at the network almost passed out. Prince Philip in Rome, Georgia. Boy, what a story!

He picked up the phone and called WRGA in Rome. The part-timer in Rome answered the phone.

The network guy said, "I need to get some audio on Prince Philip's visit to Rome."

The D.J. said, "Do what?"

The network part-timer said, "Hey, man, the Prince of England is in Rome shooting grouse with the mayor. Ain't you guys covering it?"

The man in Rome said, "Naw."

The networker finally talked him into seeing if he could find the wire copy on the story. Once he found the copy, the network part-timer said, "Look, I need some audio on this. If you will just read me the story, I'll record it and put it on the State Network."

The guy in Rome said, "Do you mean all I have to do is read this to you over the phone, and you'll put it on the network?"

"Yeah, man, that's all," came back the quick reply.

"Then my voice will be heard all over the whole state?" The part-timer beamed.

The story was read and recorded by the network.

In a few minutes, the Rome news director came back to the station to find the part-timer with a wall-to-wall smile. "Guess what?" he gushed to the news director. "I'm gonna be on the Georgia Network." He told the whole story to the horrified news director, who rushed to the phone, called the network, and had the story killed just seconds before it ran all over the state.

When it was all over, the part-timer said to the news director, "There's only one thing I don't understand. How long have we had a Communist Mayor in Rome?"

Oops!

Chris Moser was signing his show off and intended to say "This is Chris Moser, and news is next."

He said, "This is Chris Muser and Nose is next."

Program Directors

In my almost twenty years in talk radio, I have had twenty-nine program directors. They have, for the most part, been very nice people. I have enjoyed working with them, and most of them are still my friends to this day.

A program director for talk radio has a strange job. There seems to be nothing for them to do, and, therefore, there are no qualifications for the job.

I am of the opinion that since there is nothing for them to do, almost anyone can do it.

One of my P.D.'s over the years was a woman taxi driver, who was hired to direct the programming of a twenty-five thousand-watt talk radio station. She was a very nice person. She smiled a lot, and, all in all, was very bright. She always had nice, fresh flowers on her desk. I know she was my boss because about once a week she would pass me in the hall of the radio station and say, "I enjoyed your show yesterday, Ludlow." That seemed to be the extent of her involvement.

Another P.D. I worked for was a twenty-three-year-old gay Englishman. His major contribution to the radio station was to have a series of forms to be filled out about prospective guests. He somehow had the idea that it would be beneficial to make a list of all the questions you were going to ask a guest.

I don't know why he thought this was important, but he seemed to have his little heart set on it.

He did not seem to realize that the only good radio interview was one that was absolutely spontaneous. The form he came up with required that the host put down his first ten questions. I thought it was silly then, and nothing has happened since to make me change my mind.

My special guest one day was to be the world-renowned salesman and author Og Mandino. When I tried to fill out the form, I realized that it was impossible to know what questions I was going to ask him in advance. My interviews are very conversational, and I never know what my next question will be until I hear the answer to my previous question.

I thought the whole idea of canned questions was stupid, and I did not know how to fill out the form. I decided to give it all the importance it deserved, and here is what I put on the form for my first five questions:

1. When you were a child, did you get into many fist fights because your first name was Og?

2. Is Lassie an egg-sucker?

3. How far is it to Cleveland?

4. Does Zsa Zsa Gabor really wear a flea collar?

5. Did you ever deep-fry a Moon Pie?

It goes without saying that the Englishman did not see the humor in all this. He took my form right to the station manager and said, "Ludlow will just not cooperate."

The manager said, "Look, everyone knows Ludlow is crazy. Just leave him the hell alone!"

It seemed to work out because about two weeks later the P.D. quit.

I had known Larry Lowenstein for years. Larry has spent most of his life involved in show business, and when they announced that he was the new P.D. at WRNG Radio, I was very pleased.

I knew that he had no previous experience in talk radio, but he is a real idea guy, and I felt he would be a great addition to the station. Like all of the really great idea people, Larry would have ten great ideas and then come up with one so off the wall it could wrinkle a duck's feathers.

Larry had been in show business so long that he knew almost everyone worth knowing, and with one phone call he could arrange for an interview with Arthur Godfrey, Andy Griffith, or George Burns. I'm afraid, however, that when it came to his coming up with show topics, it was another matter entirely.

I'll never forget the day he came running up to my desk with a huge smile on his face. He was bubbling. He said, "Luddy, I've got this great idea for a guest." Always anxious for a good topic or a good guest, I told him to lay it on me.

He said, "You know, on TV in the morning they have a woman who is signing for the deaf, so that our deaf friends can understand what the news anchor is saying?" I nodded and he went on. "Let's book that woman on your show."

I said, "O.K., Larry. What will we talk about?"

He said, "Why, of course, Luddy, you'll talk about the obvious thing."

Puzzled, I asked, "And what is that?"

He took a deep breath and, in a very patient voice, said, "You can talk about what radio means to the deaf."

Another program director once said to me, "I had a great idea this morning, but I didn't like it."

An Atlanta program director once said, "There is too much sports in our football tailgate show."

Some of my best friends are program directors. As a matter of fact, I used to be one. But when it comes to talk radio, they are about as useful as posthole diggers indoors.

Oops!

The Atlanta Falcons play-by-play announcer said, "The quarterback is rolling out. They're after him. It's a piss out!"

Bipedal

Most of my career has been spent working days, but for three wonderful years I was on WSB from ten P.M. until two A.M. WSB is a fifty-thousand-watt, clear-channel station, and at night its signal goes all over the United States.

In my three nighttime years, I got calls from almost all of our states. Night people are a whole 'nother breed of cat.

One night I was doing "Letters to Ludlow." I wrote myself the following phony letter:

Dear Ludlow:
John and I plan to be married next month. I love him with all of my heart. He is kind,

considerate, and he loves me as much as I love him.

Until two weeks ago, I was the happiest woman on earth. Then my whole world fell apart right before my eyes.

I found out that my beloved John is bipedal. I didn't believe it at first, but, since my whole future was at stake, I did some checking, and, God help me, I found out it was true.

I'm crushed, Ludlow. I don't know which way to turn. I live in a small town, and there is just no one I can talk to about this.

Ludlow, I know your radio audience is full of understanding, loving people. I need some advice. Would you ask your audience if it is possible for a woman to find true happiness with a bipedal man?

I'll be listening. Sign me . . .

Worried in Waycross.

The dictionary defines bipedal as having two feet, but I never said that. I just read the letter, and then said, "O.K., folks. That's a letter from a lady who is in great pain. Do you have any advice? Can a normal woman find happiness with a man who is a known bipedal?"

I was not quite prepared for the response. The listeners who knew what I was doing played right along.

The first call was from a lady who said that she had been married to a bipedal man for fifteen years. She said that, for the most part, she had learned to live with it.

She went on to say that over the years he had managed to lead almost a normal life. He was even able to take up golf as a hobby.

She closed by saying that she had tried not to dwell on his condition. She did admit, however, that when he was on the golf course and she was home alone, sometimes, in those quiet moments, she wished that he was not bipedal.

We had several people to call and ask what bipedal meant. I said, "Look, I don't want to get too graphic, because this is a family show. Why don't you just get a medical dictionary and look it up?"

The advice poured in from all over the country. The most interesting tidbit came from the folks who didn't know what we were talking about.

One lady called and said that no woman in her right mind would marry a bipedal man. She went on to say that she didn't know if these men could father children or not, but wouldn't it be awful if the children turned out to be bipedal?

A preacher from Missouri called and said that the man had made a choice to be bipedal and that the woman should break off the relationship at once. In his best Oral Roberts voice, he said, "This man has chosen this life style. He has made his bed. Now he must lie in it. May God have mercy on him."

Two ladies called and said they were never going to listen to me again because they didn't want to hear all that sex talk on the radio.

The next day my phone rang off the hook all day. I heard from six different doctors, who had patients calling them wanting to know what bipedal was.

An Atlanta minister called and said several ladies of his flock had called him to complain about my show. He was very kind about it. When I told him what it meant, he said, "Why, there's nothing dirty about that!"

I said, "Preacher, the only dirt here is in the minds of the ladies who called you."

One of my favorite listeners, Roxanne, admitted years later that she had gone to the library to look up bipedal in a medical dictionary. She said she didn't want anyone to know what she was looking up, so she took the dictionary way over in the corner. When she found out what it meant, she made a silent vow to pinch off my head the next time she saw me.

I've said it before: my job is more fun than a free county fair.

Oops!

The station manager burst into the program director's office and said, "What's the matter?"

The P.D. said, "Transmitter trouble. We're off the air."

The station manager said, "Have you made an announcement?"

The Four Freedoms

President Roosevelt had just announced his "Four Freedoms." It was the talk of the country.

WJHP in Jacksonville, Florida, decided it would be a good idea to do a special fifteen-minute show on the "Four Freedoms."

The format was to be a simple one. They were going to use three announcers—one to read the intro to the show, the other two to sit side by side and, in a very dramatic voice, take turns reading the "Four Freedoms."

Just before airtime, one of the announcers took a glass, filled it with water, and set it on the table in front of him.

The "On Air" light came on, and the

announcer, in a big voice, said, "Ladies and Gentlemen, The Four Freedoms." At this point, one of the seated announcers reached into his mouth, removed his upper plate, and dropped it into his friend's glass of water.

Needless to say, the men went on to giggle their way through the "Four Freedoms."

Oops!

When the station went off the air, the manager called the chief engineer's house looking for him.

The engineer's wife answered the phone and said he was not home.

The manager said, "I need to find him. We're off the air."

The lady said, "Did you check the plug?"

The Naked Truth

Radio is a fun medium, and the people who are most successful are the ones who relax and have fun. We have a saying posted in the newsroom at WSB that sums it up: "It ain't brain surgery. It's radio."

I worked with a talk show host at WRNG who was so stuffy that he did his show in a three-piece suit. He would actually check his hair to make sure it was just right before he went on the air.

When he announced that he was leaving to take a job up North, Bob Mohan and I decided that it was up to us to give him a going-away practical joke.

We decided the way to say good-bye was to do something that would break through his stuffy armor and make him "break up" on the air. We knew that it would not be an easy job because neither Mohan nor myself had ever even seen him smile on the air.

We worked on our practical joke for days.

His last day on the air was a Saturday. The station was empty except for the producer, me, Mohan and our victim.

The poor guy didn't even know that we were in the station.

I went in and told the producer that no matter what happened, he was not to go to a commercial break.

We went into the Green Room and took off all our clothes. We stripped absolutely to the skin.

I had bought two children's watercolor sets.

When we thought the time was right, we suddenly stepped into the broadcast booth as naked as two jaybirds. Our victim never even smiled. He just continued to talk to his on-the-air caller.

We would not be denied. We took the paint sets and started to body-paint each other. Still no reaction.

We stayed in the booth for about twenty minutes, and he was so cool the audience never knew anything was out of the ordinary.

When it became apparent that we were not going to break him up, we left and put our clothes on over our paint-smeared bodies. Our joke had backfired on us.

When the show was over, we asked him how he had maintained his composure.

Without blinking an eye, he said, "I just thought of Jesus on the cross."

Some days it just doesn't pay to get naked.

Giving the formation, the football play-by-play man said, "The blacks are split."

Gorgeous George

Hank Morgan was the Sports Director at WSB-TV. He was looking for a lead story for the eleven o'clock sports. He needed a one-line tease for the start of the news.

He checked the wire and saw that the wrestler Gorgeous George had just died. He decided that his tease would simply be, "Gorgeous George is dead."

He sat down in his place, and while he was waiting for the camera to come on, he was trying to think of the best way to read the line. He decided to practice out loud.

"Gorgeous George is *dead*."
"Gorgeous George *is* dead."
"Gorgeous George is dead."

He was sitting there, mumbling that line to himself, when the camera came on. Suddenly, the whole thing struck him as funny, and, amid gales of laughter, with his whole body shaking, he said, "Gorgeous (HA HA HA) George (HA HA HA) is (WHA HOO) dead (HE HE)!"

Oops!

The announcer said, "It's thirty-nine degrees in the Windy Shitty of Chicago."

Who Died?

Any radio newsman worth his salt dies a thousand deaths when he mispronounces a word.

The following story took place some years ago at WSB. I have decided not to name the newsman involved to prevent a punch in the mouth.

He was in the middle of a news broadcast when he was handed a bulletin. The bulletin told about the assassination of Moise Tshombe, the president of the Belgian Congo.

He realized, to his horror, that he had absolutely no idea how to pronounce Moise Tshombe, and there was no time to find out. Here is what he said:

"The President of the Belgian Congo was

assassinated today in a hail of bullets as he rode in a parade in what was apparently a military coup.

"The President's name is being withheld pending notification of next of kin."

The newsman said, "The President posed later for pictures with the Iowa Republican candidates, but he did not plug them publicly."

The Elephant

Somedays nothing seems to go right for you on the radio. Just when you think you are so bright and so sophisticated, somebody is going to come along and bring you back down to earth.

About halfway through the show, a man called and said, "Ludlow, I have a riddle for you."

I said, "O.K., Partner. Let's have it."

He said, "Can you tell me what is gray and comes in quarts?"

I say, "Boy, that's tough. Let me see—What is gray and comes in quarts? What could it be—gray and comes in quarts."

I could hear the guy starting to giggle softly on the phone.

I finally said, "I give up. You're going to have to tell me. What is gray and comes in quarts?"

He said, "You really don't know?"

And I said it again—"No, I don't know what is gray and comes in quarts."

The guy said, "Elephants."

I said, "I don't get it. Elephants don't come in quarts."

By this time he was laughing his head off. He said, "Wanna bet?"

It finally hit me. It was too late to bleep out what he had said.

It took me about two years to live that one down.

Oops!

The announcer meant to say that his sponsor was having a three-for-one-cent sale.

In his best deep voice, he announced they were having a three-for-one-shit sale.

Herman T. Peavey

One of my regular callers is Herman T. Peavey. Mr. Peavey speaks in a deep voice with a soft, southern accent.

The first time he called, he announced that he was running for President. He had formed his own party called Feminist Liberation Abolitionist Party — FLAP, for short.

Mr. Peavey's position was decidedly anti-woman.

He said that the reason we had so much unemployment was because of women in the workplace.

He said that women had no business working, that they should be home looking after their lord and master husband.

He had no problem with women voting, as long as their husbands went into the voting booth with them to tell them who to vote for.

He continued to call me on the air, on and off for about a year. Each time he called, he got more and more outrageous about taking rights away from women.

It was obvious to me that this caller was pulling everybody's leg. However, after every call I would get irate calls from women who wanted to respond to some of Mr. Peavey's insanities.

I decided that, with all of the attention Herman was getting, he would make a good on-the-air guest. So I invited him to come be on with me, and he jumped at the chance.

I promoted the fact that he was going to be on. I wasn't sure if we would get any calls or not.

There was no reason to worry. The lines were full, well before airtime. Women were calling by the hundreds to rip all the hide off old Herman's back.

One lady called and said that he had no business running for President or even for dog catcher.

Herman heard her out, and then, in a very sweet, condescending voice, said, "Now listen, little missy. You got no reason to get your pretty little self all upset with all this man talk. Why don't you go on back to your parlor, watch some of your soap operas on the TV, and leave all these politics to the men?" He went on, "You seem like a sweet little thing, and I just bet you are a wonderful cook and a good housekeeper. Now, don't you trouble yourself with all this man talk."

I said, "Herman, weren't you pretty rough on her?"

He said, "No, not at all. She is probably not a bad person. Just misguided. She should realize that women should stay home and be barefooted and fertile."

He went on to say that all this women's lib foolishness was started by a group of small but well-organized ugly women. They were too unattractive to catch men, so they decided to try and enter the workplace and take jobs away from men, who were trying to earn a living for their families.

He said, "Not only did they not shave their legs, but they didn't have enough sense to be let out of the house unattended."

During the next commercial break, our news director stuck his head in the booth and said, "The lobby is full of women carrying picket signs and threatening to beat Mr. Peavey to death."

I thought he was kidding, so during the next news break, I took the elevator down to the lobby. Sure enough, there they were, picket signs and all, calling for Mr. Peavey's scalp.

When the show was over, I smuggled Mr. Peavey out of the building through the basement.

I don't know what the ladies intended to do, but it was too big a chance to take. The man who first said, "Hell hath no fury . . ." certainly knew what he was talking about.

Oops!

The network anchor said, "This airplane flies at twice the sound of speed."

Homer Southwell

Another of my exciting radio spoofs was Homer Southwell.

The idea for Homer came to me in the middle of the night. I got out of bed, found my briefcase, went to my dining room table, and Homer Southwell was born.

I thought it would be funny to have a guest on the air who was such a bigot that he hated, loathed, and despised anything or anyone from the North.

I wanted him to be such a dirty, disgusting, no-good S.O.B. that even his mother would short-sheet him if she had a chance.

Sitting at my dining room table, I decided I

needed an excuse to have him on the radio, so I made him an author who was in Atlanta on a book tour.

His first book was called *Yankee, Go Home*. He had also written a sequel called *And Stay There*.

I worked most of the night coming up with venomous lines for Homer to say — lines that would make people so mad they would call and rip all the bark off of old Homer. Some of his original lines were:

1. The best form of birth control known to mankind is a Bronx accent.

2. For entertainment, Homer said he read the *New York Times* obit column.

3. Santa Claus did not go to see the children up North.

4. Yankee women did not shave their legs.

When I had all the material put together, all I needed was to find someone to play the part of Homer Southwell.

The next day I still had not decided who would be my Homer. My phone rang, and as soon as I heard the voice on the other end of the line, I knew who Homer was going to be. On the phone from Chicago was my stepbrother, Lewis Grizzard.

Lewis told me he was coming home for the Christmas holidays. I told him about my idea for Homer and asked him if he would be the voice of

Mr. Southwell. He agreed, and I knew he would be perfect.

Not only does Lewis have a funny, quick mind, he also has the southern accent Homer needed to be believable. Lewis would make the perfect Homer.

I was going to do the spoof the afternoon of New Year's Eve.

I got to the station early to put the finishing touches on the show. About fifteen minutes before show time, my phone rang. It was Lewis. He told me that his soon-to-be ex-wife was flying to Mississippi to visit her family. She was changing planes in Atlanta, and she wanted Lewis to meet her at the Atlanta airport so they could fight. He felt obligated to go see her.

I said, "Well, Lewis, since she came all the way from Chicago to fight, I think the least you can do is go see her." He thanked me for understanding, and we hung up.

It suddenly occurred to me that I had no show put together as a backup. Not only that, because of the holiday, the radio station was empty. I walked back through the desolate station, hoping to find somebody . . . anybody . . . who could be my Homer Southwell. I went back into the sales department, and there sat one of our salesmen. He was late with his expense account and was trying to get it finished before the holiday.

I quickly explained that I was in trouble and needed him to play the part of Homer Southwell. After a little coaxing, he agreed.

I had made some flash cards with some of the lines I had written on them. The salesman was nervous, and I was nervous because he was nervous.

The "On Air" light came on, and I said a silent prayer: "Lord, get me through this and I'll quit smoking."

We went on the air, and it could not have gone better. My salesman friend turned into Homer Southwell right before my eyes.

The first caller was a man who said he was originally from Maine. In a very friendly voice, he said, "Mr. Southwell, I'm afraid I find your attitude disturbing."

Before he could say another word, Homer jumped right through the phone. He said, "I find your accent disturbing." Without giving the poor man a chance to say a word, he went on. "What the hell are you doing here anyway? Did you get tired of eating lobster and come South for a decent meal?"

After that call the telephones went absolutely crazy. We did that hour in full combat gear.

Toward the end of the hour, Homer said, "Before we sign off, I have a message I want to share with the radio audience." He went on in a very serious voice. "Do not allow your children to play with Yankee children. Teach your kids to make fun of them and to ridicule the way they talk. That way, they will not be happy here, and maybe they will put their parents under pressure to move back up North where they belong."

Homer closed by saying, "Please buy my book. Read it and take my advice. If you are from the North, get somebody to read it to you."

The fallout from the show was more than I had expected. People called the station and wrote letters for more than two weeks.

About a week after the show I received a call from Atlanta's (and perhaps the Southeast's) largest bookseller.

The lady said they had received hundreds of phone calls from people who wanted to buy Homer's books. She said, "Please promise me that the next time you're going to have an author in town who is that hot you'll call me so I can set up an autographing party for him."

You can't fool all the people all the time, but if you have your own radio show, you can come real close.

Oops!

The local announcer meant to say, "And, now, here are tonight's high school football scores."

It came out, "And, now, here are tonight's high fool scootball fours."

Jeannie

The man-on-the-street interview was a staple of local radio stations for many years. People were anxious to find a man-on-the-street microphone to talk into about local issues.

Nobody seems to know exactly why, but by the middle forties man-on-the-street interviews had become old hat. It became harder and harder to get people to talk on the radio.

Radio stations decided they would have their own street people give small amounts of money to people who could answer a question on the air.

In 1946, WJHP in Jacksonville, Florida, sent Hank Morgan out on the street to talk to people and give away a few dollars.

People were very mike-shy, and when they saw Hank coming toward them, carrying a microphone, they would walk off the sidewalk and into traffic to get away from him.

He finally cornered a real "Snuffy Smif" type. He knew the guy was not going to be an ideal interview, but time was growing short, and he was getting desperate.

Hank stuck the mike out and said, "Sir, I have a five dollar bill for you if you can give me the last word in this song title: 'I Dream of Jeannie with the Light Brown _____.' Give me the missing word, Sir, for five dollars." The man's face went absolutely blank, and his mouth was slightly open.

Hank knew he was in trouble. He tried again to get either an answer or some kind of sound out of Snuffy.

"Yes, Sir," he said with forced cheerfulness, "just give me the last word in this classic song by one of the most respected composers in American music history. The title again is, 'I Dream of Jeannie with the Light Brown _____.

"Sir, for five dollars, give me that last word." Silence. "Sir," Hank said again, "do you know the answer?"

Speaking right into the microphone, the man said, "The last time I saw her, she had a real nice pair of tits."

Oops!

The commercial should have read, "Fly the best, fly Northwest Orient Airlines."

The announcer said, "Fly the best, fly Northwest Arient Oirlines."

The Nerd

My friend Dan Fitzpatrick and I were co-hosting a show one Saturday afternoon.

Our topic was, "What is a nerd?" We were trying to find out all about nerds.

We asked, "How does a nerd dress? What kind of a job would a nerd have? Where would a nerd go to college? What kind of a car does a nerd drive? What does a nerd do for entertainment?"

We were having a great time, and the callers were into the spirit of the show and giving some very funny descriptions of a nerd.

About halfway through the show, a young man called and said, "Mr. Porch, my name is Robbie. I'm twelve years old, and I have a definition of a nerd." I knew he was serious. What I didn't know was that he was about to read me a definition out of his dictionary. I said, "Go ahead, pal. Tell me what is a nerd."

He took a deep breath and said, "Nerd: a noun. One who is uncool, a person who for one reason or another does not fit in with his peer group. Organ unknown."

I did not want to embarrass him, and I had intended to go right on to the next call. However, when he said, "Organ unknown," Dan fell on the floor, laughing like an absolute wild man. That was all it took. I went into gales of laughter. We did a commercial, came back, and were still laughing. The more we thought about a nerd having an unknown organ, the more we laughed.

This happened many years ago, but until this day, whenever I hear somebody called a nerd, I wonder if he has an unknown organ.

Oops!

He meant to say, "This message was brought to you by the Upper Midwest Council for Better Vision."

He said, "This message was brought to you by the Upper Midwest Council for Better Virgins."

The Black Santa

I have always felt that bigotry, no matter which side it's coming from, is not only wrong but also silly.

If you hate a person because of the color of his skin or the way he worships God, that means you had to start hating him the day he was born. Who in his right mind could hate a baby . . . any baby?

I refuse to judge a person by anything except his or her actions.

Since I have been doing a talk radio show, not many weeks have gone by without some yahoo trying to lure me into a serious discussion of "the racial issue." I don't like to discuss it on the radio. There is nothing left to say about it. It's boring, and I, for one, don't want to provide a forum for a bigot, be he black or white.

My attitude has only served to make both sides mad. In one single broadcast, I have been called a "closet Ku Klux Klansman" and a "nigger-lovin' Jew liberal." I am neither Jewish nor liberal, and I regard Klansmen as a bunch of hate-filled mouthbreathers.

Several years ago there was a big flap in the local newspaper. It seems that a department store had used a black Santa Claus at Christmastime. Some people had complained, and he had been replaced with a more traditional Kris Kringle. Could anything be more silly?

I received a call from a black man who was really upset. He raved about it for a few minutes and finally tried to draw me into this lunacy by asking, "What do you think about it?"

I said, "Do you really want to know what I think?" He said he did. I said, "O.K. Santa Claus is white."

Shocked, he said in a loud, angry voice, "What?"

I said, "Hold on for just a minute. You asked me a question. Let me answer."

I went on, "Santa Claus is white. Don't get mad at me about that. Everybody knows he is white. The pictures of him are all white. The whole world knows that Santa Claus is a white man."

I concluded by saying, "Look, partner, let's leave it this way. We got Santa Claus and you got Sammy Davis, Jr., and you just may have the best of that deal."

To my surprise, the caller started to laugh. He said, "You know, Ludlow, I never thought of it that way."

I said, "Come see me." He said he would. We parted feeling better about each other.

Oops!

The network announcer read the following story:

"Today Prime Minister Winston Churchill celebrated his birthday by eating a thirty-pound birthday cake along with his children and grandchildren."

Punch Lines

One of my favorite topics is "punch lines." The premise is a simple one. I tell my listeners to call and give me the punch line to their favorite joke. I think a good punch line will stand on its own.

When you hear a punch line, one of two things happens. It either reminds you of the joke it goes to, or, in your mind, you make up a joke to go with the punch line.

I have only one rule when I do punch lines: it must be clean. I don't care how filthy the joke is, as long as the punch line is clean.

Over the years we have elevated several punch lines to our "Punch Line Hall of Fame."

1. He'll bite you.
2. The one in the middle is definitely Willie Nelson.
3. Honest, officer, the midget was on fire when I got here.
4. Hey, lady! Your sign fell down!
5. What do you think this is—a duck?
6. Want a bite of my sandwich?
7. The first thing I'm going to do is get the brakes on this truck fixed.
8. Your monkey's on fire.
9. The regiment votes to repair it.
10. Paint my house.

See any of your favorites?

Oops!

The hockey announcer said, "They will sit out their penalty time in the locker room and get a jump on the other guys getting in the shower."

Amazing William

Over the years I have had several radio psychics on my show. These are the folks who can tell your future, strictly by the sound of your voice.

It sounds too good to be true, and I have always thought that it was. But my listeners disagree. Whenever there is a psychic on the air doing readings, people call by the thousands.

My theory is a simple one: I think people want so badly to believe in a psychic that they will not admit that most of the predictions are a long shot at best—and probably impossible.

I've always heard, "If you can't lick 'em, join 'em," so I decided to invent my own fortuneteller.

My friend Tom Deardorf showed up to play the

part of "The Amazing William." I had five other setups on hold before we even went on the air, and they were going to be my first five callers. I told them to agree to whatever "The Amazing William" told them and to act like they were amazed by the accuracy of his so-called "reading."

When the show went on the air, I said my special guest was the foremost psychic in the world. I went on to explain that he could tell you about your past, present and future. All a listener had to do was call and give William his first name, his birthday and his shoe size.

I went to my first set-up call. It was a lady who wanted William to help her find a very expensive antique ring that she had lost.

William said, "Is this a ring with two large diamonds and seven smaller diamonds?"

In great surprise, the caller said, "Why, yes, as a matter of fact, it is!"

William said, "Do you live in a white house with blue shutters?"

The caller said, "Yes."

In a very serious voice, William said, "Go to your linen closet. Look on the second shelf. Look in the stack of hand towels. You will find your ring on the third towel from the bottom."

I said, "Go look, Ma'am, and we'll hold on."

She was gone about thirty seconds. When she came back to the phone, she was squealing with excitement. "It's a miracle! It's a miracle! Oh, William, how can I ever thank you?"

The next call went pretty much the same way.

William told the caller, "I can tell by the sound of your voice that you are a second-shift mechanic for Delta Air Lines."

"That's right," the caller said, in mock surprise.

By the time we talked to our five set-up calls, the hook was set. The switchboard was jammed, and for the next few minutes we talked to a lot of people who didn't seem to think it was strange that William needed their shoe sizes before he could tell them their fortunes.

We were careful not to give any serious advice to the serious callers.

Several callers asked William how much he charged for a private reading. He told them one hundred dollars, which included a six-month warranty. Nobody bothered to ask what that meant.

When there was about five minutes left in the show, I said, "Ladies and gentlemen, I have a confession I want to make to you. This entire radio show has been a lie." I said, "The Amazing William is really my friend Tom Deardorf." Turning to Tom, I said, "Tom, do you have any psychic powers?"

Chuckling, Tom said, "Of course not. The whole thing has been a joke. I don't know anything about the future and darn little about the present."

I said, "Ladies and gentlemen, I want you to remember this show the next time you are tempted to give your hard-earned money to a so-called psychic."

I might as well have been talking to myself. The telephone lines were still jammed with people wanting to have their fortunes told.

When the show was over, I went back to my office thinking that I would hear no more from my psychic show. It's a good thing I'm not a professional psychic, or I'd starve for sure. The P.A. system at the station was going crazy. "Ludlow, line one." "Ludlow, line two."

I thought the calls would be from people wanting to complain about the show. Instead, they were from people wanting to know how to reach William for a private reading.

I said, "Don't you understand his name is not William and he is not a psychic? He is a phony. The whole show was a joke."

They all said the same thing. "Yes, I know, I heard you say that on the radio, but I still want a reading."

I said, "And you're willing to pay one hundred dollars?"

They all said they were and wanted his phone number, in spite of the fact that I had told them all that it was a spoof and a lie.

I made several people very angry because I would not give the telephone number of "The Amazing William."

People continued to call for about a month. I received calls from other radio stations that were trying to reach William.

I really don't know what kind of conclusion we can reach from this, but one thing does seem to be clear: people believe what they want to believe, and they really, really want to believe in psychics.

Oops!

The WSB announcer said, "This was the first regularly scheduled crash of a Southern Airways jetliner."

LeRoy Fong

If you do a talk show long enough, you are going to have trouble from time to time coming up with a topic that you are pleased with.

One day I had rejected about ten topics when I finally hit upon this idea: I decided to invent a person and see what my audience would tell me about him.

I went on the air and said, "Well, today is the day that we have picked each year to honor Leroy Fong. I want to find out about your memories of Leroy Fong. Give me a call and tell me your favorite Leroy Fong story, or give me your favorite Leroy Fong trivia questions. I would also like to hear from some of you who collect Leroy Fong memorabilia. If you ever had the pleasure of actually meeting Leroy, give us a call."

Here are some of the things we found out about Leroy Fong:

1. His middle name was Ping.
2. He was the first man to ever eat Wheaties mixed with Diet Pepsi.
3. He was the first man to produce a situation comedy with no cast.
4. Leroy invented camouflage deodorant.
5. He was the first man to throw himself on a hand grenade and then go to a Ferlin Husky concert.
6. It was reported that he was the first man to ever faint twice in Providence, Rhode Island.
7. He invented the phrase, "No Shoes, No Shirt, No Service."
8. Leroy invented shower curtains.
9. He was a graduate of Florence State College.
10. He invented the first welcome mat that said, "Go Away or I'll Kill You."
11. He was once married to Dorothy Kilgallen.
12. He invented the game of Cowboys and Indians. Before that, he invented Cowboys and Rocks.
13. While living in Columbus, Georgia, he invented the world's only kerosene-powered guitar.

14. He once sang first tenor in the First Baptist Church Choir in Moultrie, Georgia.
15. He was the M.C. at the Eugene Paulette and Sterling Holloway Film Festival.

We talked for two hours about the mythical Leroy Fong. I'm not sure I know what that means. I do think, however, that it would indicate that folks will talk about dang near anything.

Oops!

The commentator referred to the Joint Chiefs of Staff as "the Chief Joints of Staff."

Flip-Flop Parade

The Flip-Flop Parade was the brainchild of Kitty Litter, one of the whackos who has been around my show about as long as I have. She has a quick mind, and she thinks funny. She lives in Tucker, Georgia, and is Tucker's biggest booster.

One day we were talking on the air, and the subject of flip-flops came up.

I explained my theory about them: "Flip-flops are tacky, and only tacky people buy them. I don't know how many generations it will take before the human race realizes that feet are ugly, and any shoe that shows your whole foot is ugly.

"Not only that, but take a look at the next person you see wearing flip-flops out in public. You will quickly see that you are dealing with major league, top of the line tacky."

Kitty listened while I went on and on about flip-flops.

On my birthday a few weeks later, Kitty gave me a pair of charcoal gray flip-flops with a matching necktie.

Every time we talked on the air for the next few months, the subject of flip-flops seemed to come up.

One night while we were having dinner together, Kitty suggested that it would be fun to have a Flip-Flop parade in "beautiful down-town Tucker."

Kitty wrote a script, and Miller Pope (my friend and probably the best talk show producer in the business) put together all the sound effects we would need.

The idea was to make it sound like we were doing our broadcast live from the parade route. We wanted it to sound like we were really there, describing this non-existent parade.

We ran promos for the parade for days in advance.

It was to be on Labor Day, and, since it was the Flip-Flop Parade, we announced that everyone in the parade would be wearing flip-flops and all of the spectators would also be wearing flip-flops. As a matter of fact, we said that the police had set up check points and would not allow anyone to come into Tucker unless they were wearing flip-flops.

We had many calls before the big day, wanting to know exactly where Kitty and I would be broadcasting. Fans wanted to stop by and visit. We announced we would be broadcasting from in front of where the post office used to be.

We have done the Flip-Flop Parade several years now, and there are thousands of people who think there really is such a parade. Kitty's scripts are funny and believable. She packs the parade with big names. Our first Grand Marshal was Mikhail Baryschnikov. He was followed the next year by Slim Whitman.

Our "Twelfth Annual Tucker Labor Day Flip-Flop Parade" started with our announcer, in a very dramatic voice, saying, "And, now, from the world's next great international city, Tucker, Georgia, zip code 30084, AM-750 WSB is proud to present the twelfth annual Labor Day Flip-Flop Parade, dedicated to the memory of Madame Florence Foster Jenkins." (Madame Jenkins was a would-be opera singer from New York that nobody ever heard of.)

The tribute to Madame Jenkins was kicked off by former Georgia Governor Lester Maddox singing, "I'll Fly Away." Governor Maddox was followed by the Tucker High School Marching Band playing "Seventy-Six Trombones."

We then had hundreds of men, women and children pass by, all wearing flip-flops. The sound effect was perfect.

Slim Whitman was there, wearing his famous red-sequined cowboy suit and riding his horse. As Slim passed our broadcast spot, he was singing "Rose Marie."

The famous Tucker Tomato Truck was also in the parade. Pete Rose was on the back of the truck, signing tomatoes and selling them to his fans in the crowd.

Julio Iglesias and Willie Nelson came by on a float, along with all the girls who had wandered in and out of their door.

The winners of the Industrial Waste Look-Alike Contest, Tommy Lasorda and Don Rickles, came by in a convertible.

Former Surgeon General C. Everett Koop was there with a sign on the side of his convertible that said, "Say No to Everything."

Not everyone in the parade was famous, however. We had many local Tucker businesses represented. For example, there was a float from Mr. Sonny's Hair Care and Front-End Alignment Salon. As the float passed, we announced that on the float Mr. Sonny was doing a complete makeover on Tammy Faye Bakker. We said that when Mr. Sonny was through, Tammy Faye would have only one set of eyebrows.

There was a float from Darlene's Instant Fat Removal Clinic, with a sign on the side that said, "Fat Removed While You Wait."

There was a float from Bubba's Sushi Bar, Bait Shop and Yogurt Parlor.

Another float was from Sick People's Hospital in Tucker, complete with a replica of an emergency room and real doctors and nurses.

I guess my favorite float of all was the one that carried people who had met while dialing the 976-Let's Whoopee party line. This float featured Rob Lowe holding a video camera.

Doing the phony parade on radio has been great fun, but the reaction has been unbelievable. People have driven from miles around to see and enjoy the parade. One Georgia State Patrolman heard us on the radio and actually drove to Tucker to see if he could help out with traffic and crowd control. When he called me on the air to tell me what he had done, I told him that since he was not wearing flip-flops, they wouldn't have allowed him in town anyway.

One lady told me that she had wanted to bring her family from Rome, Georgia, to see the parade, but they didn't go because there was no place to buy flip-flops in Rome.

Members of the Tucker Jaycees actually got mad with us because they felt our phony parade was taking away from their Tucker Days Parade.

Most people knew that it was all in good fun and took it all in good form.

As of this writing, I have received over one hundred requests for tapes of the show. I have been contacted by numerous organizations who want to be in next year's parade, including one U.S. Government organization which shall remain nameless.

I guess all this proves only one thing—everybody loves a parade, real or imagined.

Oops!

The Chicago radio announcer said, "Windy this afternoon, with snow and occasional dribble."

The Chattahoochee

One day I had my friend Tom Deardorf on my show posing as the owner of an oil company.

I introduced him as John Brickhouse, President and Chief Executive Officer of the Timberline Oil Company out of Waco, Texas.

I explained that the Timberline Oil Company had discovered oil under the Chattahoochee River. It was under the stretch of river that went through one of Atlanta's fanciest residential areas.

We talked about the fact that oil was where you found it, and if America was ever going to be independent of Arab oil, then we must take oil out, no matter where it was.

Then we dropped the bombshell. We said that Timberline was going to start drilling in the middle of the river the following week.

We went on to explain that there would be huge oil rigs over a twelve-mile stretch. We said the oil would be put in fifty-gallon drums and floated down the river to the I-285 bridge, where men would fish the barrels out with long poles.

We said that I-285 would, of course, have to be closed down weekdays from eight A.M. to five P.M.

We had several calls from people who were just curious and asked some interesting questions. Then the call came that I knew would kick the show off to a running start.

I had told Tom before we started the show that the first really critical call we got, I wanted him to jump all over the caller. And believe me, nobody does that better than Tom Deardorf!

I said, "Go ahead. You're on the air."

The caller said, "I am a friend of the river."

Before he could take another breath, Tom said, "Yes, by God, and I'm a friend of the automobile. Let me see you take that stinking river to work some morning. You bleeding hearts are bringing America to its knees and causing the oil shortage!"

The caller screamed out, "You're going to kill our wildlife!"

Tom was all over him again. "Yeah! We're going to kill some fish. So what? Do you know anybody who fishes the Chattahoochee for a living?"

The caller was so mad he was almost in tears. "What about the rafters?" he asked.

"What about them?" Tom said. "I can't believe you're really worried about a few yuppie sissies floating down the river. If we're going to whip the Arabs, you and your yuppie sissy friends are just going to have to suck it up."

The caller was starting to hyperventilate when I cut him off.

The next caller was a Fulton County commissioner, who said, "I'm an elected official, and this is the first thing I've heard about this. Do you have a permit?"

Tom said, "My permit comes straight from the White House." That seemed to satisfy him.

Another screamer called and said, "We're planning a protest."

Tom said, "Don't get your head busted."

Some of the listeners who knew what we were doing called and agreed that it would be good for Atlanta to find oil in our area.

One man pointed out that derricks in the middle of the river would be a great tourist attraction.

One well-meaning lady called and said, "They should paint the derricks green. Maybe they wouldn't look so bad."

We received phone calls for about two weeks, and I received over five hundred pieces of mail.

I learned a lot from this spoof—mainly that people are not apathetic when it comes to the Chattahoochee.

Oops!

When Durwood Kirby was a young radio announcer, he was given a script that was to be read after a local show went off.

The line he was to read said, "The preceding program was brought to you by the Bond Bread Bakers."

The line came out, "The preceding program was brought to you by the Blonde Bed Breakers."

The Arabs

Of all the spoofs I've done over the years, I have had to admit to only one on the air.

My friend Tom Cooper was my partner in crime. I introduced Tom as a man who was worried about the Arabs taking over Cobb County, the bustling county northwest of Atlanta.

We told about a little known Georgia law that had been passed in 1860. The law simply said that whenever one entity, be it person, organization or corporation, owned two-thirds of the property in a given county, then the county became theirs.

We revealed that over the years the Arabs had been quietly buying up very, very expensive real estate in the county, until, at long last, they owned enough real estate to take control of the whole ball of wax.

We said that plans were under way to convert several local churches into mosques. We talked about the fact that thousands and thousands of Arabs were on their way to take possession of the county. They were bringing camels, harems and tents.

The first clue I had that we had gone too far was when people started to call from Cobb County. Some of them were crying, and all of them were upset beyond words. The whole county was up in arms.

When we were about thirty minutes into the show, the station manager came into the booth. He was all blue around the lips.

He had received several calls from Cobb County bankers. People were going to the banks and taking their money out before the Arabs took over.

It was apparent to me that I had screwed up bad. I asked the station manager how he wanted me to handle it.

He said, "This is your baby. Don't get me involved in it."

I went back on the air and said, "Hey! This was a joke. We're only kidding. Leave your money in the bank." That seemed to calm the situation down.

144

The Next Sound

The call came about five minutes before I was to go on the air. Normally, I don't take any calls for about an hour before airtime, but something just told me that this call was important.

His voice was flat. There was no emotion. I said, "Hello."

He said, "Ludlow, the next sound you hear will be me blowing my brains out."

I could tell by the sound of his voice that this was not a crank caller. This was a man in such pain that he didn't want to live. This was a man so alone that he had to call a stranger to spend his last seconds with.

I was terrified. I fully expected to hear a shot

any second. I knew that whatever I said I had to say it quick.

I blurted out, "You gutless sonofabitch!"

Startled, he said, "What?"

I said, "Who gave you that right?"

He said, "What do you mean?"

I said, "Partner, tell me about it."

He told me a story about his wife leaving him and taking their son.

It was not a new story, but it was sad. He sobbed through the whole story. When he finished, he said, "Tell me what to do, Ludlow."

By this time, there were tears in my eyes. I said a silent prayer, "Dear God, let me say the right thing."

I said, "Look, I don't know if your divorce was your fault or your wife's fault, but I do know that it wasn't your little boy's fault. If you kill yourself, do you realize—do you have any idea of—the legacy, the memories you will be leaving your son?" I said, "You just don't have the right to do that."

He said, "I'm at the end of my rope. I don't know what else to do."

I said, "Look, pal, you've been through this for weeks. A couple more hours is not going to make any difference. Let me come talk to you."

He said, "I'm afraid you'll call the police if I tell you who I am."

I said, "All you have to do is give me your address, and when I get off the air, I'll come to your house, and we'll talk this out." He finally agreed and gave me his address. I left it on my desk.

While I was on the air, our news director found it and called the Suicide Prevention Bureau. Their advice was that I not go. The theory was that many suicides think that when they die they go to a better place. And oftentimes they want to take someone they like with them.

I explained to our well-meaning news director that I had promised my caller that I would be there, and as soon as I was off the air, I was going to the man's house.

While I was doing my show, the news director called the police and told them what was going on. The police sent two officers to the man's home. One of the police officers was also a minister.

When they arrived, they looked through the window, and my caller was sitting in a chair with a gun across his lap and another on a table beside him.

They were able to get him to the door and take him to a mental health facility without incident. The officer/minister was not only a loving, understanding man, he was also trained to handle situations like this.

When I found out what had happened, I tried to go see my caller but was not allowed to see him.

Several months went by before I heard from him again. He called to thank me and to tell me that he was fine and had handled all his problems.

I still hear from him from time to time. He has a great, warm relationship with his son. He and his ex-wife did not get back together, but they are now friends.

I have never met my caller face to face, but I look forward to his calls. He is one of my many, many friends that I have never met.

I have the best job in the world.

Oops!

The sports announcer only had about ninety seconds for his whole sports show, and he was hurrying to get all the scores in.

The whole show came to a stop when he called the New York Yankees "the New Yank Yorkees."

Stop Reading

An Atlanta all-news radio station employed a news guy who never wrote any of his own copy. He either ripped it right off the wire machine or somebody typed it up for him.

He was not real popular with his co-workers because he was somewhat of a prima donna.

One day a practical joker typed his copy up and gave it to him. Like always, he did not read it ahead of time.

What he didn't know was that, midway on the second page, the joker had written, "Stop reading here, asshole."

You guessed it. He just kept right on reading.

Oops!

There had been several Civil Rights demonstrations in Atlanta.

The newsman meant to say, "Dark clouds are gathering outside WSB Radio."

What came out was, "Dark crowds are gathering outside WSB Radio."

For a few minutes the world thought WSB was being picketed.

The Stars

When you interview a star for only one hour, you get certain impressions about the people on the other side of the mike. Some of the folks I have interviewed became my friends. Most of them I never saw or heard from again. Here are my impressions after spending an hour with some of America's biggest stars.

SHELLY BERMAN

Generally speaking, I like everyone until they give me a reason not to.

When Shelly Berman sat down in the studio for my interview with him, I knew immediately that we were not going to be friends. He is a mean-tempered man who thinks he is much funnier than he is.

The first thing he did before we went on the air was to make fun of my producer's haircut. I thought that was a little strange, since Berman was wearing a rug at the time that made him look like he had a dead chipmunk on his head.

He has a brilliant sense of humor, but his wit is very acidic. It seemed to me that he took great pleasure in putting people down.

The interview lasted an hour. When it was over, he signed my guest book as follows: "Dear Ludlow, This has been the most boring hour of my life."

I went to see the play he was in that night. When my wife and I got home from this very bad play, I called Western Union and sent Mr. Berman the following telegram: "Dear Mr. Berman, I caught your play tonight. Now we're even."

GODFREY CAMBRIDGE

Godfrey Cambridge was the first black stand-up comic to talk about race and race problems. He did it with love and great good humor. I am convinced that he paved the way for Richard Pryor, Eddie Murphy, and a host of other young black comics.

Godfrey was in town to plug a movie. The interview with me was to last only one hour, but we were both having so much fun that it went on for two hours.

That first meeting started a friendship that lasted until the day he died.

Godfrey spent most of his time on the road, either making movies or doing dinner theater. This meant that when he was doing dinner theater, he was alone in a strange city with nothing to do all day. He was a pretty lonely guy and would call me from all over the country just to talk and catch up on gossip.

Of all the friends I have made through my radio show, none was closer than Godfrey.

BOB HOPE

Bob Hope was in town at a local department store to autograph his newest book.

The radio station made arrangements for me to go down and tape-record an interview for later broadcast.

When I walked in, Mr. Hope had just finished signing hundreds of his books. We talked a minute and he said, "Before we start the interview, I need to go to the bathroom."

He left for the bathroom. When he was through, his P.R. people hustled him out of the store to his next appointment, and I never saw him again.

The story of my life—beaten out by a commode.

LEE MAJORS

When the network P.R. people called and wanted to have Lee Majors on my show, I was pleased. I had been a fan of "The Big Valley" and was anxious to meet and talk to one of its stars.

When "The Big Valley" had gone off the air, Majors had signed almost immediately to do a show called "The Six Million Dollar Man."

I was doing my show at that time from the middle of a giant shopping mall. The station had built a very nice, soundproof booth. We had promoted the fact that Lee Majors was going to be our guest.

"The Six Million Dollar Man" was a huge network hit. I have never quite understood it, but the show had a great appeal to a very young audience.

About an hour before showtime, a crowd started to gather to see our guest. The network folks had even sent out some pictures of "The Six Million Dollar Man" in action. Most of the crowd were mothers with three-, four-, five- and six-year-old children.

When Lee Majors arrived, he was led right through the crowd to the broadcast booth. He didn't speak to any of the mothers or the children. He never even looked at them, nor did he in any way acknowledge that they were there to see him.

He came into the booth with one of the P.R. guys. I stuck out my hand, smiled, and said, "Welcome." He was not smiling.

He didn't say, "Hello," "Thanks," or "Kiss my foot." He looked me right in the eye and said, "How in the hell did you arrange this freebie?"

I said, "I beg your pardon?"

He barked back, "What are all these kids doing here?"

I said, "They came to see you."

He said, "I usually get $6,000 for a public appearance, and you're getting this free." That remark pushed me right over the edge.

I said, "Listen, Buster! I didn't arrange anything. Your people called me and asked me if you could be on my show. If you've got a problem, take it up with your people, and, in the meantime, get out of my face!"

By this time, we were both shouting. The network guy got between us. Turning to me, he said, "He'll be all right. He'll be all right."

I said, "No, he will not be all right, unless he sits down and shuts up."

We both knew that a fist fight in front of all those people would not be a good idea, so we both sat down. He turned to me and said, "How long do I have to stay?"

I said, "You can go now." Once again, the P.R. guy acted as peacemaker.

The interview was to have lasted an hour, but, due to the strained nature of our relationship, I wound it up in twenty minutes.

When it was over, Majors stood up and left. He didn't say a word. He walked right through that crowd of children and never slowed down. He never spoke or looked at any of the people who had come to see him. In about thirty seconds he was out of the mall and gone.

About six months later, Peter Breck was my guest. Mr. Breck had been one of Majors' co-stars on "The Big Valley." When the show was over, he invited me out to lunch. While we were eating, I told him about my meeting with Majors. He laughed and said, "Don't let it bother you. He thought he was a big star before anybody knew who he was!"

Peter Breck assured me that Majors was not one of the more popular stars on "The Big Valley" set.

I was pretty upset, however, when I didn't get a Christmas card from "The Six Million Dollar Man."

ANDY GRIFFITH

There has never been a bigger Andy Griffith fan than me.

I first heard of him when he was known as Deacon Andy Griffith. The year was 1952 or 1953. He had just made a record called, "What It

Was Was Football." I thought he was the funniest newcomer to hit show business in years.

I didn't hear anymore about him for awhile, and then I read that he was a big hit on Broadway in "No Time for Sergeants." I took some pride in his success since I had been a fan of his almost since day one.

He followed "No Time for Sergeants" with several hit movies and was no longer known as "Deacon."

One night I was watching "The Danny Thomas Show." It was about Danny driving through the South. He came to a town called Mayberry and was, of course, stopped by the local sheriff. I was amazed to see that the sheriff was played by the friend I had never met, Andy Griffith.

What I didn't know at the time was that I was watching a pilot film for "The Andy Griffith Show."

When it was announced that the network was going to start "The Andy Griffith Show" in the fall, I was happy as Zsa Zsa Gabor in a divorce court.

I loved the show from the first episode. In a short time, I felt like Mayberry was my hometown.

I knew all the townspeople. I knew Barney so well that he felt like a relative. I loved Aunt Bee, Gomer, Floyd the barber, and Clara Edwards.

I knew that no matter what kind of problems would pop up in Mayberry, Sheriff Andy Taylor would use his love and his wisdom to solve them.

In short, I was an Andy Griffith groupie.

When the network folks called and asked if I would like to have Andy on my radio show, I almost jumped through the phone. The show had been off the air for awhile, but, like the rest of America, I was still watching the reruns.

When he arrived at the station, he was taken into the Green Room, a sort of waiting room. He was traveling with seven or eight people, and they were falling all over themselves to help him, bringing him water, coffee and everything else they could think of.

I took him into the studio to wait for the news to conclude so we could start our interview.

He kept getting up and going back to the Green Room to give instructions to his people. He seemed to be having a little trouble with his speech.

Then it hit me. Sheriff Andy Taylor was drunk! My first thought was, "Dear God — not Opie's daddy — not Bea's boy!"

The interview went well, and I don't think anybody in the audience ever knew that he had a few pops before the show.

I found out later that he had been to a press luncheon before he came to the radio station and had apparently been over-served.

During my off-the-air conversation with Mr. Griffith, the only thing he wanted to talk about was his career and what he was going to do next.

Andy Griffith was O.K., but I got to tell you the truth—I liked Andy Taylor a whole lot better.

DON KNOTTS

I guess one of my biggest surprises came when I interviewed Don Knotts.

I think Barney Fife was one of the finest characters ever to be seen on TV, or anywhere else, for that matter. I somehow thought that Don Knotts would be that same type of outgoing person.

Nothing could have been further from the fact.

Before we started the interview, he smiled and said, "I will be glad to answer all of your questions, but I think you should know that I can't ad lib with you."

He went on to explain that he was not a very funny person by nature. He said that he was just an actor who read other people's lines.

He said that he tried to put together a night-club act, but that it had never worked out because he was just not very funny. He also said that live audiences were not his cup of tea.

It was apparent that he was uneasy being on the radio.

He said, "I'm just an actor, and about the only roles I ever get are those of a nervous, funny man."

I really enjoyed my hour with Don Knotts. He is a dear man.

DON AMECHE

Mr. Ameche is a warm, grandfatherly type who really enjoyed talking about his past. He seemed amazed that I was as familiar with his career in radio as I was.

He was in Atlanta to do a play. I asked him if, after all these years, he still enjoyed all the traveling it took to take a play on the road.

He smiled and said in that beautiful voice, "Ludlow, I'm too old and too rich to do it if it wasn't fun."

I liked Don Ameche a lot.

VIRGINIA MAYO

Miss Mayo had been a big star in the late forties and fifties.

She seemed a little sad. Once, when I asked her about her late husband, actor Michael O'Shea, tears came to her eyes. She was nice, but it was obvious that she would rather have been somewhere else.

She seemed to be overly concerned about her age. She would not allow anyone to take her picture.

MEL TORME

Mel became my friend. He is a very, very talented man who enjoyed being on my show. The night after our interview, my wife and I were his guests in his hotel suite. He was the perfect host.

Whenever he is in town, we talk. He is hard-working, and, even after all these years, he loves show business. Mel is a real people person.

GLORIA DeHAVEN

Gloria danced into America's hearts in the forties' movies. We had lunch together after the show. I loved Gloria DeHaven.

PAUL LYNDE

The late Paul Lynde just may have been the funniest man I ever interviewed. He showed up for our eleven A.M. interview smoking a cigar and drinking straight vodka out of a paper cup.

VAN JOHNSON

A super nice man. He referred to himself as an aging star. He really enjoyed talking to his fans on the radio. He was very down-to-earth and answered every question, no matter how personal, with great good humor. He kissed my wife's hand and made her day. Van Johnson seemed to be a very happy man with no regrets about his life or his career.

CLORIS LEACHMAN

I didn't like Cloris Leachman. She is plain-spoken to the point of being rude.

She could not resist looking at my ample waistline and saying with a sneer, "How could you do this to yourself?" Miss Leachman is only pleasant when the mike or the camera is on her.

I said in a previous book that she had a bitchy streak as wide as Waco, Texas. Looking back on it, I'm sure I was giving her the benefit of the doubt.

RICH LITTLE

What a talent this man is! When his fans called and asked him to do different impressions, he did every one they requested. He is a very nice man that I would like to know better.

GUNILLA KNUDSEN

Gunilla is a former Miss Sweden. You will remember her as the beautiful lady who did the "Noxzema" shaving cream TV commercials for a long time. The camera would be on a man shaving to the music of "The Stripper." She would look into the camera, and in her sexy, Swedish accent, she would say, "Take it off. Take it *all* off."

She was in Atlanta plugging a massage product called Rose Oil. She said she would like to give me a massage on the air.

163

I (being a good host) agreed. She said, "Strip to the waist." I said, "From which end?" It was a good interview.

Later that day I got Lewis Grizzard a date with her. About five years later, she was on my show again. Lewis came by to see her, and she did not remember him. That surprised me. I was even more surprised that Lewis did not ask her to marry him.

CHARLTON HESTON

Charlton Heston had just written a book called *The Actor's Journal.* When his publisher called to ask about him being on the show, it took me about eight seconds to say yes.

I greeted him in the Green Room. I extended my hand and said, "Mr. Heston, I'm Ludlow Porch." He said, "Call me Chuck." I couldn't believe how nice he was. We talked for an hour about his book, his life and his career.

About ten days after he left, I received a nice letter from him thanking me for having him on and inviting me to come see him when I was in California.

Once he called my home, and my sixteen-year-old daughter answered the phone. She had no idea who she was talking to until he said, "Please tell Ludlow that Chuck Heston called."

She was almost struck dumb. Shortly after she talked to him, the long distance operator called and asked my daughter if she would mind telling her who had just called. My daughter said, "You ain't gonna believe this!"

When you are on the radio, your kids pretty much take it for granted. But when Moses calls you at home, you suddenly get more respect.

PAT PAULSEN

Pat and I became friends after about ten minutes. He is in person exactly like he is on stage — quick, funny, and seems to like everybody.

I sat in a bar with him one night, and he kept me and everybody else laughing for two hours.

Pat is one of my favorite people.

MERCEDES McCAMBRIDGE

If there is a better actress in the world than Mercedes McCambridge, I don't know who it is. One of the best things that has come out of my career in radio is my friendship with her.

She is a lady who has really had a tough, roller-coaster life. She won the Oscar for her first movie, "All the King's Men." She had a drinking problem for many years. She won that battle and no longer drinks.

She was a major network radio star long before she ever made a movie. And she is quick to say that radio is her favorite medium. She has a wonderful, warm personality.

I may be wrong, but I think she is a little like Will Rogers. I don't think she has ever met anybody she didn't like.

FANNIE FLAGG

Fannie is a good old girl from Alabama who has never forgotten her southern roots. I have interviewed her several times. She is a very funny lady.

There is no way to be around Fannie long without falling in love with her.

RICHARD SIMMONS

I was never a fan of his until I met him. What a wonderful, wild little man he is. He has enough energy to light up the whole state of Rhode Island.

He cares about people. He wants everybody on earth to feel as high on life as he does. Richard Simmons is a special man and a good friend.

KIRK DOUGLAS

Mr. Douglas was about three-fourths bombed when I interviewed him. He was nice enough, I guess, but I got the impression that he was not giving me straight answers. I think he was there to make himself sound as good as he could. There is nothing wrong with that, but I didn't feel that I knew much more about him after our interview than I did before.

E. G. MARSHALL and ELI WALLACH

I interviewed these two fine actors together. Nice men, who both puffed on huge black cigars the whole hour we were on the air.

RAYMOND BURR

The characters that Raymond Burr has played over the years have always seemed a little gruff to me.

He is not that way at all. He is a smiling, laughing, giant of a man that I really, really liked.

We talked about his career and his life in general. He has a home on Fiji that he loves more than anything. He spends his spare time there. He invited my wife and me to visit him on Fiji. Boy! Wouldn't that be something!

FORREST TUCKER

The late Forrest Tucker had been a favorite of mine since he played a bad guy in the old B-westerns. I enjoyed him in many of the John Wayne movies, like "Sands of Iwo Jima." I watched and enjoyed his comedy in "F Troop."

When I met him in the Green Room, his first question was "How long before we go on the air?"

I said, "About twenty minutes."

He said, "Let's go out and have a drink."

I told him I didn't think there was time. He seemed desperate for one and finally sent one of his people out for a bottle. The whole time we were on the air, he was drinking straight bourbon—no chaser, no ice. He was a good guest, but it was apparent that he had a problem.

He called me several days later while he was pretty high and invited me to come have a few drinks. I was busy and had to decline. I never got to see him again.

SAM LEVENSON

I hope people still remember the late Sam Levenson. He was a hugger. I interviewed him two or three times. He was not only a warm, funny man, but he made you wish that he was your uncle. Sam Levenson was one of my favorites.

SID CAESAR

Mr. Caesar was a pretty boring guest. He was pleasant enough, but it was pretty obvious that he was anxious to be out of the studio and on his way. He seemed very nervous. I was glad when our interview was over.

IMOGENE COCA

What a delightful lady! Funny, charming, and quick to laugh. She seemed to have a good time, no matter where she was or what she was doing. A dear lady I could have talked to for hours.

168

CAROL CHANNING

Yes, she really talks that way. Carol Channing has a way of making you think you are the only other person on the planet. When you talk to her, she locks her eyes onto yours, as if she can't wait to hear your next word.

She was on the air one hour, and everyone in the radio station fell in love with her.

TED MACK

Mr. Mack became a national celebrity in the early days of TV doing "Ted Mack's Original Amateur Hour."

When I booked Ted Mack, I thought, "This is going to be a great show! Here is a man who was right there when television was a baby. This man will have more great stories than anyone!"

I knew that he not only discovered some show business legends, he also did more live TV shows than almost any other person. He was going to be the world's most interesting guest!

Boy! Was I in for a surprise.

He gave me one-word answers to all my questions.

I said, "I guess those early days of TV must have been pretty exciting."

He said, "Yes, they were."

I said, "How long did your show run?"

He said, "Oh, ten, twelve, fourteen years— something like that."

I said, "What brings you to town?"

He said, "We're doing a show over at Georgia Tech."

All his answers were just that way. No matter what I tried, I just could not draw more than two or three lines out of this gentleman.

Finally, I said, "Mr. Mack, what's the funniest thing that ever happened to you on live TV?"

He said, "I guess it was the time, my hair caught on fire."

I thought to myself, "Boy, oh, boy. I'm finally going to get an interesting story out of him."

Trying to give him a chance to launch into a funny story, I said, "Your hair caught on fire?"

He said, "Yeah, my hair caught on fire." No explanation, no nothing, just, "Yeah, my hair caught on fire."

I said, "How did that happen?"

He said, without a trace of emotion, "The lights were too hot."

I said, "Mr. Mack, I hope you enjoy your stay in Atlanta, and thanks for coming."

The whole interview was over in less than ten minutes. It had been a nightmare.

Two weeks later, one of our newsmen stuck his head in my office and said, "Did you hear? Ted Mack just died in New York."

I said, "That makes him two for two."

Oops!

When you read the same weather forecast over and over, it can get boring, so you try to come up with new ways to make it sound different.

One radio announcer had talked several times about how bad the fog was. He meant to say, "The fog is as thick as pea soup." What he said was, "The fog is as thick as sea poop."

Matriculating

One day I wrote myself the following "Letter to Ludlow" and read it on the air:

Dear Ludlow,

I am outraged. I just found out that in the City of Atlanta school system, grades one through twelve, our children are being required to matriculate every day in school.

I am very upset. Please read this letter on the air and see if we can't get something done about this.

Angry in Atlanta

When I had finished reading the letter, I said in a very solemn voice, "What is this world coming to?"

The first caller said, "Why, Ludlow, all that means is . . . ." Before he could finish, I cut him off and said, "Come on, now. We have to keep it clean. We can talk about this like adults."

I took several more calls. Some of them understood what I was doing and some didn't.

Then one of those dream calls came in. It was a man who said he was calling from just outside Montgomery, Alabama. I could tell by the serious tone of his voice that he had swallowed the bait.

He said, "Ludlow, did you go to school in the Atlanta area?"

I told him that I did. He said, "Were they doing that in school when you went?"

I said, "I'm not real proud of it, but I think they were probably doing more when I was in school than they're doing now."

He paused, took a deep breath, and said, "I went all through school in Montgomery, Alabama, and I will guarantee you one thing. If they were doing it there, they were doing it in the bathroom."

The more he talked about it, the more upset he became.

I finally said, "I don't want you to be too upset about this because survey after survey has shown that there is less matriculating going on at the University of Alabama than at any other major college in the United States."

That seemed to make him feel better.

Sometimes we all need to pause and think about who we issue driver's licenses to.